HANDBOOK OF PROFESSIONAL TOUR MANAGEMENT

Robert T. Reilly

Merton House Publishing Company, Wheaton, Illinois

ISBN: 0-916032-18-3

Library of Congress Catalog Card Number: 82-81356

Merton House Publishing Company
937 West Liberty Drive
Wheaton, Illinois 60187

Manufactured in the United States of America

*To my wife, Jean,
and the miles we've
shared together*

Contents

Foreword

Tour management is a rewarding profession with unlimited opportunities to travel. The travel industry is expanding dramatically and is now the fastest growing business in North America. Years ago, travel was considered a luxury; today it's more a way of life. Increasingly, people have more leisure time and more money to travel, and they are spending billions of dollars to visit new places. This recent upswing in travel has created an unprecedented need for people who are trained as professional tour managers and local guides, for both domestic and international travel. Tour operators need qualified people—now more than ever. They are looking for a select number of creative individuals who like to work with people, enjoy traveling, and want a challenge. They need people they can trust with the responsibility of professionally providing the services and standards demanded by the client and by the company. There are not enough trained and experienced people to fill this need.

Despite the current emphasis on individualism, on doing one's own thing, and despite the media image of tours (*If This Is Tuesday, It Must Be Belgium*), tour packages remain a staple of the travel business. It is just for this reason that the tour manager is a necessary part of *every* tour. The role of the tour manager is to professionally alleviate the many frustrations encountered by the traveler.

The profession of tour manager is perhaps one of the most rewarding in the world. Travel . . . See new places . . . Visit places of historical importance and interest . . . Meet new people, say the headlines. In reality there is much more to deal with.

Handbook of Professional Tour Management will provide an understanding of the tools one needs to succeed in this fast-growing career. It formally introduces the prospective tour manager to the field, and explains the skills necessary to succeed as a professional tour manager. Robert Reilly provides detailed information regarding the duties, background, and qualifications of tour management on land, air, and sea.

Pierre J. Bouchier
International Association of Tour Managers
New York

About the Author

This is Bob Reilly's second book for Merton House, the first being his best-selling text on *Travel and Tourism Marketing Techniques* published in 1980.

Reilly's nine other books, fiction and non-fiction, cover a wide range of topics, from the Indian Wars to a textbook in public relations. Many of his books have Irish themes, including *Come Along to Ireland,* which combines a tour through Ireland with glimpses of the country's history and culture, and *Red Hugh, Prince of Donegal*, which was made into a Walt Disney film in 1966. Reilly has also published over 400 articles in a variety of national magazines, writes poetry, scripts films and TV shows, and has produced material for Mike Douglas, Fred Waring, and Capitol Records.

A native of Lowell, Massachusetts, Reilly now lives in Omaha, Nebraska, where he's a professor of communication at the University of Nebraska at Omaha, teaching courses in advertising, public relations, and advanced writing.

The author spent 30 years in the advertising-public relations field before returning to teaching on 1972. During these years he worked on travel accounts in Boston and Omaha, served as public relations director for Creighton University, and was a partner in Holland Dreves Reilly Inc., the state's largest home-based advertising-public relations firm.

Bob and his wife, Jean, an account executive with one of America's ten largest travel agencies, have led numerous tours, with Ireland and the British Isles ranking as their favorite territory. Reilly has also traveled widely in Europe, the South Pacific, and the United States—first as an infantryman in

World War II, and later as a public speaker or on film assignments.

Reilly has a masters degree from Boston University, where he also spent two years toward his doctorate in English.

He's been a consultant to the Ford Foundation, provided counsel to numerous commercial and nonprofit agencies, and once lost a close race for Congress.

His honors include a number of foundation grants; the Fonda-McGuire Best Actor Award at the Omaha Playhouse (1954); Hall of Fame Award from the American College Public Relations Association (1965); Boss of the Year Award in Nebraska (1969); Midlands Journalist of the Year (1977); and the Kayser Chair at the University of Nebraska at Omaha in 1979.

Reilly is listed in *Who's Who in Advertising*; *Who's Who in Public Relations*; *Who's Who in the Midwest*; *Contemporary Authors*; *The Dictionary of British and American Writers*; *Dictionary of International Biography*; *The International Writers and Authors Who's Who,* and *Writers and Photographers Guide.*

Introduction

"I don't see how you can teach someone from a book."

That was the response of one tour operator when queried about this proposed text. In a way, he's right. All you can do in a book is set out some principles, provide a few examples, and incorporate a checklist. After that, it's up to the tour manager.

Leading a tour is like teaching a college class. The material may be familiar but the audience and circumstances invariably differ. In each class, or on each tour, you have new people and new chemistry and a new environment. You never know what you are going to face until you embark. Reading about possible problems, or even hearing about them, doesn't really register until these difficulties become your own.

"If I were there, would I know what to do next? That's the question."

Another questionnaire respondent wrote those words. And that is the test. You plan to the best of your ability and then you improvise. The list of possible situations is endless. This volume merely traces the routine surface, with a few excursions into the more bizarre occurrences.

An attendant risk in setting down specific guidelines is that many tour leaders have developed their own special methods, their own unique reactions to emergencies. Consequently, there will be differences of opinion. As with advertising, there are myriad solutions to a single challenge. The pragmatic evaluation must always be: Does it work?

Because there seems to be a shortage of practical literature about tour leadership, Larry Stevens of Merton House asked me to compile this volume. It is based on the experience of my wife and myself as tour

1

managers, as well as on dozens of personal interviews, mail questionnaires, and tips gleaned from a variety of printed materials. It is aimed, primarily, at those who are new to tour escorting, or who wish to polish up their techniques. Even for the experienced escort, it may serve as a ready-made checklist, a quick method of determining that all is in order.

Some 150 survey forms were mailed to a select list of tour operators and escorts. Forty responded and completed the questionnaire. A few replied that they were too busy; some mentioned that their experience was too broad to be confined to a few pages; some demurred, fearful of revealing trade secrets. One respondent misread my purpose and assumed I wanted to be a tour escort, thereby assigning me some courses and books.

To those who took the time, who did condense what they knew, who were willing to share information, I am most grateful. These individuals are: Barry Johnston, Rev. Richard Linde, Countryside Community Church; Loretta Cutler, George Dinsdale, Mal Hansen, Lawrence Youngman, Ro Trent, Travel and Transport; Julie Brown, Katie Sackett, AAA; Allied Travel Inc.; Shepherds Tour & Travel Inc.; Barbara Angell Leonard, Discovery Tours; Leone A. von Weiss, The Hamilton Travel & Incentive Corporation; Margaret A. Potteiger, Freelance (Westours, Green Carpet Tours etc.); M. Schaipfer, Touropa International, Inc.; Darrell Vincent, Tower Travel; Garth Peterson, Bon Voyage; Nadine Morrow, Travel Faire; R. W. Woody Hefner, Hefner Tours; Eleanor Woods, On the Scene; David A. Davidowitz, Vagabond Tours for the Deaf; R. Postean, Trade Wind Tours; Ruth Fein, Rambling Tours; Alana Fried, Born Free Safaris; Hal Mischnick, North American Tours; Genevieve Smith, Kneisel/Green Carpet Tours; Bob English, Peter Travel; John Hlavacek, TV Travel; Maggie Moreland, Brandeis Travel; Charles Kissane, Freelance; Robert L. Peck, World Wide Travel, and a number of unsigned respondents.

I'm particularly grateful to Mrs. Janey Ashley, who assisted me with the survey, with interviews, and with additional research, and to John Fogarty for helping with the proofreading.

1

The Tour

Touring is hardly a recent invention. People have been involved in this diversion since the beginning of recorded time. Their motivation then was, no doubt, similar to that of today's travelers. They sought a change of scenery, adventure, an escape from boredom, an educational experience, a better climate, and the chance to meet people, make visits to relatives or friends, even do some shopping.

Individuals banded together for safety, economy, companionship. They had their leaders, individuals who knew the territory or spoke the language or who had demonstrated managerial qualities. Pharaohs sailed the Nile; Romans trekked to medicinal spas and distant arenas; Phoenicians made a career of travel and bartering; the early Britons journeyed to a chain of religious shrines, giving rise to inns and taverns en route. Such groups employed guides who merely got them there and back, sans microphone or cocktail party.

Beginning in the 18th century, it became fashionable for the wealthier English people to do the Grand Tour of Europe. No education was complete without it. Men and women, from wastrel gentry to diary-carrying females, took months, even years, to cover the itinerary of today's three-week excursion. France, Germany, Switzerland, Spain, Italy, Greece. Oliver Goldsmith and Lord Byron and Maria Edgeworth and Lord Chesterfield. They wrote letters and memoirs, recommending some amenities, panning others.

In some cases, the trip was organized, but not in today's parlance.

Thomas Cook, who stares at us from the traveler's checks he (along with

American Express) may have initiated, is credited with being the world's first bona fide tour leader. In the 1840s, smitten with the cause of prohibition, Cook began chartering trains to transport himself and his colleagues to distant temperance meetings. Later, this imaginative Englishman branched out, scheduling trips through a quartet of European nations, cruises on the Nile, and luxury rail journeys into exotic India. His son, John, supervised tours through newly-opened Yellowstone Park and across Civil War battlefields in the American South.

The Cooks also produced the first travel brochures of note, itineraries for passengers, and vouchers to expedite the payment to suppliers. The senior Cook scored another first in 1872 by personally circling the globe. It took him 222 days.

Others followed. Thomas Bennett, a former British consul, entered the travel agency business in 1850, and became a forerunner of Fodor and Fielding by publishing standard guide books. On this side of the ocean, Ward G. Foster inaugurated a chain of travel agencies, starting in St. Augustine, Florida, nearly a century ago. His "Ask Mr. Foster" slogan ultimately appeared on seventy-five agency windows or doors.

Today there are more than twenty thousand travel agencies doing business in the United States, and their total sales volume is more than twenty billion dollars. Virtually all of them are in the tour business, directly or indirectly, although some embrace rather narrow specialties. Even where business or independent travel constitutes the major share of an agency's income, tours remain the symbol of the industry. Tours incorporate color and romance, along with anticipated profits and attendant headaches.

Why Do People Take Tours—Or Agencies Handle Them?

Despite the current emphasis on individualism, on doing one's own thing, and despite the media image of tours ("If this is Tuesday, It Must be Belgium"), tour packages remain a staple of the travel business.

Why do people go on tour anyway? Some people couldn't make it any other way. They couldn't cope on their own and they realize it. Others, while competent to tackle a journey solo, want to be free of hassles, want to have others attend to the details. Still others seek companionship. Near the end of a European tour, a group of Americans were dining together and one asked what aspect of the trip had pleased the others most. They catalogued scenes and plays and meals and accommodations. One man, a bachelor physician, said, "For me, the best part of the journey was getting to know all of you." And he meant it.

Tours provide comfort and safety, especially in countries where the language and customs are strange, or the political situation volatile. The members feel more secure with an experienced tour manager or leader. Other motives for group travel are economy of time and money, the assurance of decent accommodations, the educational aspects of intelligent commentary, and the availability of some destinations only through such tours.

For travel agencies, tours, while admittedly risky, offer an opportunity for wider profit margins. Agencies can build in profit in addition to commissions. Tours also enhance the image of an agency and give them something exciting to advertise. They lend a universal image. Tours also offer agency personnel an opportunity for leadership experience. Larger agencies, of course, organize more of their own tours, while smaller ones have to be content with a diet composed primarily of tour operators' offerings.

Tours Bear Many Titles

Like tourists, tours also come in various shapes and sizes, with a choice of titles and themes. With deregulation a fact, other names and other package ideas will certainly surface, but here are some of the general categories at this writing:

Group Tour: A tour composed of one or several groups of individuals using charter or scheduled transportation.

Charter Tour: A tour based on the chartering of equipment by a wholesaler, tour operator, individual or group, to achieve lower fares.

Affinity Tour: Not as prevalent today as in the past, this type of tour is offered to individuals with a common identity, such as membership in a club or organization.

Package Tour: A tour that encompasses land costs, some meals, accommodations, and special events, plus an escort. Carrier costs, like air fares, may or may not be included.

You also see terms like "consolidated tours," where individuals team up with already established tours; "incentive tours," where the trip is a reward for some achievement, such as corporate sales; "FIT" (Foreign Independent Travel), which may embrace an individual travelling alone on a specifically prepared itinerary or a group operating out of a single travel agency on an itinerary developed in conjunction with a wholesaler, and other variations, from convention extensions to business/pleasure excursions.

Tours may also be classified according to purpose or destination. Some of these classifications are educational, ethnic, scenic, photographic, agricultural, historical, religious, adventurous, scientific, health-related, recreational, romantic, or cultural. Their themes are limited only by the organizer's imagination. Places like Hawaii and Las Vegas and the Caribbean focus on repetitive features—exotic settings, bright lights, or a change of climate. But we also have The Chocolate Lover's Tour of Switzerland; deluxe wine tours featuring world-famous vintners; rambles through Dracula land; tours designed to see the Passion Play, or the Olympics, or a royal wedding; root-tracing expeditions; riverboat excursions; gambling forays; raft trips on the Colorado; Love Boat spinoffs, theatre tours of London and New York; or golf and tennis vacations; seasonal journeys to cherry-blossom Washington or powder-packed Aspen; youth-oriented getaway trips; and even tours built around Mount Saint Helens and other Pacific Coast volcanoes.

There are companies that specialize in tours for the handicapped, carefully selecting hotels designed for easy access, or offering escorts who speak sign language. And there are other firms whose tour specialty is the city tour, centering on conventioneers or casual tourists.

All of these packages have their own organizational and promotional techniques, their own language, and their own problems. The job of the tour manager varies with each set of circumstances, and few men or women would be adept at handling every specialty.

Modes of Travel

Travel by air is the predominant method of tourist travel, both in terms of passenger miles logged and money spent. Even though there has been a renewed emphasis on leisurely travel, most tourists prefer to spend the time at their destination, rather than getting there.

Air charter travel has rebounded from a brief slump caused by fuel surcharges, sudden cancellations, the dampening effects of inflation, concerns about equipment, and low fares on scheduled airlines. Today, fuel prices are more stable, discount fares on scheduled airlines have ebbed, and many airlines have discontinued or curtailed flights to certain destinations. Consequently, charters have a new life, particularly to the standard resort areas like Mexico and the West Indies.

Charter operations depend on near-capacity seating and practice efficiencies like back-to-back scheduling, whereby an airplane drops off a group of tourists beginning their vacation in one destination and then picks up another group concluding their vacation. To attract tourists, charters are more reluctant to cancel, and they often throw in meals, drinks, and movies as part of the package. Some charters feature air only, while others offer complete land amenities. Mass purchase of hotel accommodations and certainty about departure dates enable charter promoters to offer substantial savings.

Scheduled airlines are, of course, more reliable, and they also offer a wider variety of dates and times to the traveler. For larger groups, most airlines will also offer dollar incentives, and will provide other assistance, from block seating to personal attention at gateway cities.

Motor coach travel is another major source of tourist transportation. In the United States there are ski trips, Fall Foliage Tours, cross-country runs and other vacations that rely solely on the bus. Abroad, the air passenger is likely to be met by a bus at the airport and this vehicle becomes the sightseeing outlet. Many bus companies vie for the tourist dollar, from government-sponsored giants to small independents. The coaches themselves may be self-contained, with toilet facilities or bars, or they may be serviceable for touring only, with ample window areas to allow near-perfect viewing.

Cruise ships are now experiencing a new popularity, for they feature the most relaxing way to travel. Their selling point is the pleasure of the journey itself, with excellent cuisine, ample recreation, and a hint of romance. Some lines offer a combination of ship and air transportation. Their destinations may be insular, such as the Greek Islands or the inland passage to Alaska, or they may be extended round-the-world cruises with numerous ports of call. More frequent sailings, lush appointments and facilities, and the popularity of TV shows like *Love Boat*, plus a return to a more relaxed lifestyle, account for the current appeal of sea (or river) travel.

Trains were once *the* carrier. In Europe they remain a strong contender for vacationers, but their role has diminished in the United States. There are some attractive train packages using items like the Eurailpass or, for foreign visitors to our shores, the American counterpart. Trains also have their own form of romance, particularly lines like the Trans-Siberian Railway or the rapid Osaka-Tokyo run. It used to be like that in the United States, and Amtrak continues to offer some exciting rides, although the scheduling is much more restricted.

Other forms of transportation include everything from private touring cars and limousines to tramp steamers and hydrofoils. Some tours offer self-drive options, rented bicycles, camel caravans, rickshaws, and rafts. It all depends on the territory, the time, and the amount of adventure one desires.

The Future of the Tour

For reasons cited earlier, tours will always be a popular vacation option. Perhaps hostels, bed and breakfast places, and inexpensive hotel options offer some savings and add a touch of excitement, but things like service, location, individual bathrooms, telephones, porters, television, room for entertaining, and privacy are usually missing. Advance payment is ordinarily required on the bed and breakfast route, and credit cards are rarely accepted. Advance bookings are essential and arrival times have to be carefully scheduled.

There are many more people who swear by tours than there are those who swear at them. So the rules may vary, the prices may rise, and the destinations expand, but the advantages of group touring will always find acceptance.

2

Planning the Tour

The Destination

Many tours are getting a bit worn at the edges. Some agencies have pet areas to which they return annually; others are content to merely latch on to the popular and traditional vacation spots. There's nothing wrong with this, but variety adds spice to touring as well as life.

Certain locales will always have appeal. Hawaii, the Caribbean, the capitals of Europe. And yet today's traveler is often looking for something "different," something he or she can experience and later tell others about. Perhaps it's merely one or two new wrinkles in an old standby trip, or it could be a fresh idea, or a rarely-visited nation.

When Bhutan opened its border to tourism a few years ago, a number of agencies discovered a ready list of clients eager to be first. When Chinese tours also became a reality, one agent booked his quota in 24 hours—with one piece of direct mail, a few phone calls, and word of mouth.

A Chicago tour operator pioneered out-of-the-way spots by introducing air-conditioned vehicles to East Africa and by augmenting the few hotels on Easter Island with facilities in private homes. The same operator takes visitors to Patagonia, pre-Incan villages in northern Argentina, New Guinea, Marrakech, and Tierra del Fuego.

Obviously, these tours are not everyone's cup of tea, but they do remind us that there are many places to see and things to do that lie outside the typical itinerary. Look at the way tours—some tours—are promoted today. The sexual innuendo seen in many print ads today would have been taboo thirty years ago. With a freer lifestyle now prevalent, tours cater openly to the mating instinct, featuring everything from heart-shaped, mirrored tubs in the Poconos to bikini beaches in the Caribbean. Other tours strive to present some unusual facets. A hydrofoil cruise, a treehouse sojourn beside a jungle oasis, or a three day trail ride into the Superstition Mountains. People-to-people itineraries reflect the interest in closer ties with other nations. Folk music and art have been replacing the heavier cultural attractions. Many tours are built around sports and hobbies, piggy-backing on the interests spawned by dozens of special circulation magazines.

What the careful planner must do is try to anticipate future demands of a fickle public. Roots, mythology, romance. There are unlimited possibilities. Some are risky; some are dynamite. But caution is the key. Just because a tour of the villages of Great Britain and Ireland seems charming to the experienced tour operator doesn't mean a price-conscious, first-time tourist will want to forego the glamor of London, Dublin, and Edinburgh. Think out the drawbacks *before* announcing a tour. Hindsight is accurate—but expensive.

Setting the Dates

Intelligent scheduling is a combination of factors, some of them uncertain. You're looking for the right place at the right time for the right people and at the right price. To come up with this combination, several items require consideration. Setting the best dates depends on these.

CLIENT PREFERENCES

Depending upon your assessment of the potential clients, you'll want to ascertain good and bad times for these groups. Teachers are best bets for summer or Christmas forays; parents with small children will opt for vacation months; CPAs find it hard to get away during tax time; farmers are stronger targets in winter than in spring or fall; office staffers still lean more heavily toward traditional vacation times; students are limited by class schedules; most people want to be home for important holidays, like Christmas and Yom Kippur. The trick is to pinpoint your audience and then consider all aspects of their lifestyle and occupational routines, trying to capitalize on the most propitious seasons.

WEATHER

Weather becomes a factor in two ways. Travelers often flee their most unpleasant seasons for better weather, trading winter for summer, summer for spring. In addition, planners have to consider weather at the destinations. South Seas resorts have their dry and rainy seasons; England has its raw and mild months. Then, too, some people are chasing snow while others are eluding it. Guide books provide some general help in ascertaining likely weather conditions, but the charts of average temperatures give you only broad parameters. Since most of these statistics are provided by tourist-conscious staffs, they tend to accentuate the positive. The best course is to discuss your routing with a reliable wholesaler or with someone who knows the country in question. They'll tell you if the temperature registers fifty but feels like thirty, and if the annual average rainfall is concentrated in one month.

No tour can guarantee good weather, but it makes no sense to program for mist and misery.

SPECIAL EVENTS

Occasionally the tourist may want to avoid special events. Such events mean crowds and higher prices, causing delays and cramped facilities. If tour planners have customers who want the spirit of Mardi Gras, then they work toward it; if not, they should book earlier or later.

Most of the time, however, you want to build in some activities that add lustre and entertainment to the tour. Oktoberfest; the Galway Bay Oyster Festival; the opera season in Milan; the Kentucky Derby; Oberammergau's Passion Play. Most nations supply brochures listing principal events of the year and chambers of commerce or tourist bureaus dispatch similar materials for cities. Wholesalers are also a source of such information.

These events must be balanced against considerations such as time, cost, crowds, and the appropriateness for certain target audiences. An elderly group won't be partial to a rock concert at London's Palladium, nor will avid shoppers vote for two days at the London Horse Show. For a two week tour, a few major attractions, a few minor ones, and a handful of options should more than suffice.

COST

Although price is usually factored in after the variables are known, overall consideration of cost may disclose some initial handicaps. Some tours, though attractive, come with such high price tags that they don't prove feasible for the clientele of certain agencies. In any tour, planners must begin by assuming there must be profit in the venture. This is true of prepackaged trips as well as specially designed ones. If profit seems doubtful, a more marketable tour might be selected.

SPACE

Travel agents know—or should know—when certain areas are crowded and likely to be overbooked. Expect rooms to be tight during the Cannes Film Festival, or the New Orleans Mardi Gras, or a bowl game, or a coronation.

If planning time is short, it's foolish to embark on tours into these areas, particularly if tourists are to be promised Class A accommodations. Better to shift the scene or wait until next year.

The wise agency also keeps its regular clientele in mind and won't risk losing them because of marginal housing. Recently, when a football team was chosen to represent its state in one of the minor bowl games, many of that state's travel agencies backed off on selling tours because they felt the host city's accommodations were inadequate. Rather than field a ton of complaints, they preferred not to market the tours.

LEADER'S AVAILABILITY

If the tour leader is a part-time or occasional leader—a minister, teacher, TV personality—he or she may not be available except at certain periods. Tours have to be built around their leaders' schedules. Even with the professional tour leader, other commitments have to be considered.

THE AGENCY'S OWN OPERATION

Travel agencies rarely have time on their hands; they are busy shops. As a result, any new enterprise has to be weighed against the agency's ability to deliver. You can't tie up a small staff on a single tour; neither can you add so many tours that you don't properly promote any of them. Moderation is the watchword. Handle whatever can be efficiently, profitably managed, and give only cursory attention to the others.

Even where the bulk of the promotion and selling, and all of the details, are being handled by a national or international tour operator, the small agency still has to ask itself just how much time and money it can spend on behalf of that tour, or how cluttered it wishes to make the office sales program.

Organizing the Itinerary

In terms of volume, most tours are prepackaged. They have lavish folders and drop-in ad copy. Their itineraries and tour personnel are set. All the travel agency has to do is review the literature and, perhaps, request some alterations. Then come promotion and selling. Agencies which put together their own tours have many more problems.

DISTANCE AND GEOGRAPHY

Americans have never been too proficient at geography. Even travel agents, who should be global experts, frequently fall short in this category. In making itineraries, however, there is little margin for error. This means you must calculate distances with accuracy, considering all facets of the journey and terrain, and not merely counting inches in an atlas. If you schedule a six-hour bus trip between Point A and Point B, arriving in time for a meal and a play, are you certain you can make it? Are you able to work in all the scheduled stops en route? Are you putting too much of a burden on passengers by asking them to travel long distances in a single day?

Wholesalers may be helpful here, reminding you when you have over-extended yourself, but they are not infallible either. Many of them stick to traditional routes, and deviations from this pattern may be both unfamiliar and unwelcome to them. You should know yourself just what can be comfortably covered within the time frame you've set.

On a bus tour crossing the Great Plains you may cover 500 miles or more a day, but this is no guideline for Europe or Africa. Sightseeing opportunities and road conditions enter in. Two hundred and fifty miles can be a long day, particularly with lunch and rest stops.

Put together something that is reasonable, with longer and shorter touring days, plus some two- or three-night stopovers. This gives people a chance to catch up on their rest and laundry. Fight for what you want from wholesalers, but don't be stupid about it. If they say you can't get to Perth in four hours, they may just be right.

SPECIAL EVENTS VERSUS FREE TIME

Tourists generally expect some activities to be provided for them. They don't want to spend three successive nights in an outlying village with nothing to do but count the limited traffic.

On the other hand, you can overdo the entertainment bit. Some tours have people going all the time. Everybody out for shuffleboard! Tonight, *The Merchant of Venice.* Is everyone set for the moonlight picnic? Sitting at home, drafting the itinerary, it looks great to have all those salable attractions but, on the scene, you can watch travelers wilt. They'd appreciate a quiet night in their hotels or a chance to see and do something on their own.

Balance, that's the program. Combine a few group sessions with some free time options. Perhaps a play, a pub crawl, a tour of a winery, a ballet, a lake cruise, native dancing, all tempered with suggestions for individual enter-tainment.

Some people love night life, others loathe it. Some want to experience exotic cuisine while their companions are more timorous. Giving them personal choices takes away the feeling of being constantly herded, and it also frees up the tour manager for record keeping, making contacts, or catching up on rest. Experience dictates some procedures. Many tour directors advise giving fewer options to older travelers. Plan more group functions and allow some restful evenings. Experience also tells you to blend entertainment features that are popular with those that may be a bit highbrow. Ballet is for some folks; folk dancing is for others.

SHOPPING

Even though sightseeing will be nominated as the chief pleasure in traveling, only the foolish planner will neglect to schedule ample shopping time in the right places. This means organizing arrivals and departures properly, avoiding holidays and half-holidays, and building in sufficient free time so that bargain hunters don't feel hurried.

Certain cities are a must for shopping, but even on tours to destinations where there are no world-famous marts, tour members still want an opportunity to find something special for themselves, or collect souvenirs, or purchase gifts for family and friends. On a two-week tour, travelers will expect a couple of good shopping days along with periodic short stops.

Wholesalers and their local representatives will help with suggestions for these brief stops en route—at crystal factories or linen outlets or native arts and crafts shops.

LOCATION OF ACCOMMODATIONS

Tour planners can't always secure the kind of accommodations they seek in exactly the right places. The earlier you book, the better selection you have. You end up with Class A hotels instead of places with limited privates baths, diminutive towels, a handful of coat hangers, poor lighting, and no in-house restaurant. When you have to change locales in order to get satisfactory facilities, this may mean that some entertainment will have to be shifted or eliminated, and that some tours may require alteration.

The hotels should be spaced so there is some equity in the miles traveled daily, but also with an eye toward the attractions available in that area. Staying outside a big city may be more economical and restful, but it also curtails opportunities for shopping, browsing, sampling restaurants on one's own, and other pleasures.

REST AND LUNCHEON STOPS

These may not appear on the itinerary or in the brochures, but tour managers have to think about them. Even in the more civilized and highly-populated countries, adequate rest stops and lunch stops are not automatic. Some forethought is required. Obviously, certain tours and regions demand more caution than others but, in plotting the itinerary, it is always wise to have some notion of the most likely locales for breaks. Experienced drivers and couriers are helpful in making such decisions. And there are guides—like *American Road Guide East* and its counterparts—that even list fast food chains at each interstate exit.

TOUR MEMBERS

Solid itineraries also reflect the makeup of the tour members. Youth hostels or their equivalents are no lodgings for older citizens. Camera bugs will demand more frequent stops; a wine tasting tour can't be rushed; a farm tour must be loosely programmed.

Handicapped persons may have to forego some of the more rigorous excursions, although one travel agent recalls a man in a wheelchair who inched himself up the myriad steps of Blarney Castle, sans chair. The more elderly are susceptible to fatigue and shouldn't be expected to tolerate a succession of long driving days. Minor illnesses are more common in this age group and things like meals are more important to senior citizens—particularly the experience of sharing a meal together. On the other hand, many tour leaders swear that the older person is the best traveler.

Even the political situation may be related to audience characteristics. An older group may be more concerned in a crisis and less able to react quickly. One escort also remembers his difficulty in evacuating a Jewish group in Cairo during the Sinai conflict.

BUDGET

Some economies may be practiced in routing, accommodations, and activities without cheapening the overall tour. A play by an amateur group in an intimate setting may be more fun than occupying poor seats at an indifferent performance in a crowded metropolis. Some perfectly good hotels may offer reduced rates while building their reputations. And everyone knows that the highest prices don't always indicate the best restaurants.

From the agency's and the leader's viewpoint, however, it would be a mistake to try to go second class. Stateside tourists think this sounds exciting and democratic but, when exposed to such conditions after a long day of touring, the passengers get surly. Life becomes much easier for those in charge when complaints are minimal.

Every item you add to the itinerary affects the budget. A medieval banquet—add $25 or $30 per person. Tickets to a London play—add $15. Then there are yacht cruises, private limousine tours, pub crawls, elegant oriental cuisine. All of these items increase the tour price. Some are necessary; others may not be. The successful planner balances appeal against the affect on the total cost of the package.

Pricing

Booking tours isn't supposed to be a nonprofit operation. There are times when an agency might send off a marginal tour just to retain the company's image, but too many repetitions of this can be suicide. The intent is to make money.

Many tours regard fifteeen tour members as a minimum. This has, in the past, been the cutoff point for free escort tickets. Other packages require a minimum of twenty-five. Mel Dultz, president of Travcoa, says they'll operate with as few as ten persons and write the loss off to advertising. Obviously, the more people, the more profit, but numbers also mean other headaches and, perhaps, a dent in the company's reputation.

When assessing the proposed tour costs and attendant budget, one must be conservative. All charges have to be listed; there should be no hidden fees or expenses. Know the time limits for required deposits and for an accurate count of tour members. Be aware of any hotels that demand payment before departure. Consider the competition from similar tours. Weigh your anticipated promotional costs—advertising, direct mail, telephone, special gatherings. Try to assess the current business climate and what it might be at tour time.

Planners should also pay attention to the likely course of inflation, and to the economy of the destination country. The power of the dollar fluctuates. It gained in Europe in 1981, but lost elsewhere. Israel's skyrocketing inflation rate has influenced travel there. Canada has remained a good bargain. What the tour planners must do is figure out how things are NOW and how they are likely to stand in the near future.

Figuring air fares is a science all its own. Someone calculated that there are forty ways to figure air fares to Europe—and that's conservative. Exasperated tourists have had the experience of calling airlines and travel agents and compiling a totally confusing list of fares. The trend has been for fares to increase—as much as fifty per cent in the past few years—and the special economy packages have diminished. With deregulation, many of the traditional ways of carrier pricing may change and agents will have to learn to live with this chaos.

In establishing the tour price, the agency manager feeds all the data into a computer or cost sheet, averaging out expenses, taking all legitimate mark-ups, calculating commissions, and adding on a factor for other expenses and profit. The goal would be to realize a profit of ten to fifteen per cent. Some tours do better than this; many do worse. When you get down around seven or eight per cent you have to ask yourself if it was worth it.

To help with the profit line, many agencies have added tour items that can be marketed along with the trip. These include insurance, maps and guide books, luggage, foreign currency packets, adapter plugs and converters, and some emergency services. Some 1,500 agencies have their own Miniportrait cameras from Polaroid, which sell for under $700, and they use these to supply color passport photos.

Agencies have to protect themselves. It makes no sense to back a losing tour until it drains both profit and principal. It's also a mistake to forget about the expenses of the tour leader, plus money for extra entertainment and emergencies. Having someone else review your cost accounting isn't a bad idea, particularly when you are new to this routine.

Using a Wholesaler

It's possible of course, to deal directly with carriers, hotels, restaurants and entertainment centers—but this is a lot of work and hardly worth the effort. An article in *Travel Weekly* (April 13, 1981) compared the profitability of the packaged bus tour with the independent itinerary and concluded that the packaged tour resulted in higher agency commissions (with immediate payments), plus less work, and a lower price for the client. This comparison assumes that the independent itinerary is also booked through a wholesaler.

As a matter of fact, almost every tour relies on wholesaler input, expertise, and labor. When the travel agency manager wants to put a tour together, he or she submits a rough itinerary to several wholesalers for their bids. As in any business, getting several bids is sound policy and enables you to make a selection based on cost, services, and company reputation.

Certain wholesalers have near-impeccable reputations and the agency is pretty safe in dealing with them. Periodically, *Travel/Holiday* magazine polls its readers regarding their choices of carriers, hotels, tour companies, and other travel items. In their January, 1980, survey, for example, Maupintour, Cartan, and Lindblad were the top three mentioned by readers, with familiar names like American Express, Olson, and Thomas Cook appearing in the top ten. These companies specialize in the package tour. Independent tours have a variety of choices—with dozens of companies vying for the business in Great Britain alone.

It also makes sense to examine some of the smaller wholesalers about whom good reports circulate. Anxious for new business, they may extend themselves even more than the giants. Larger wholesalers do have more clout, at least in most situations, and they may have stronger claims on specific hotels or chains. But they can also get careless and sloppy and lose the personal touch they once possessed. They may also be more intractable than the smaller company. One considers these things when reviewing bids, augmenting that information with personal calls or letters, plus a check of clients or references.

Other Sources of Itinerary Information

Reading old itineraries, or wholesaler itineraries, or package itineraries, or competitive itineraries provides clues to forming an independent travel schedule. Materials may be garnered from tourist boards, carriers, hotels, embassies, libraries, guide books, international travel groups, and the comments of agency personnel and verteran travelers. Familiarization tours are supposed to be used for this purpose, to gather details on destinations. Conscientious agents file reports when they return, establishing a catalogue of materials for their colleagues to draw from.

The most dangerous thing to do is guess about any aspect of the itinerary, or to act on sketchy information. Before anything is offered to the public, the tour planners should satisfy themselves that the item is as represented and that it meets all the tour standards.

Coordinating the Package

When you go through a tour operator and merely advertise that tour for your clientele, the details are pretty well set. Your people enlist for what is offered.

If you go the route of organizing your own itinerary with the aid of a wholesaler, there's likely to be some give and take before the journey is finalized. Sightseeing, hotels, and entertainment must interlock. Geography and pace must be reviewed. When these variables are properly positioned, the itinerary may be committed to brochure form. The tour is then registered with the carrier and given an IT (Independent Tour) number and is ready to be promulgated.

AerLingus
Irish Airlines

TRAVEL AND TRANSPORT'S

ALL IRELAND TOUR

with

BOB REILLY

May 10 - May 25, 1981

DATE	PLACE	ITINERARY 105-19 ONE PAGE NO. 1

Sunday
May 10
	OMAHA
	CHICAGO
	NEW YORK
		Leave Omaha by United Airlines flight #304
		        9:25 A.M.
		    Arrive Chicago 10:37 A.M.
		Change planes.
		    Leave Chicago by United Airlines flight
		#252 11:30 A.M.
		(Lunch aloft)
		    Arrive New York (John F. Kennedy)
		        2:28 P.M.
		Change planes.
		    Leave New York (John F. Kennedy) by Aer
		Lingus flight #104 8:00 P.M.
		(Dinner and breakfast served aloft)
		
		        IRELAND

Monday May 11	SHANNON	Arrive Shannon 7:05 A.M. Driver and motorcoach will be waiting after customs for the transfer to the hotel. FITZPATRICK'S SHAMROCK INN Balance of the day at leisure. This evening depart for Knappogue Castle built in 1467 where highlights include a superb 15th Century Banquet and the music and song of the elegantly gowned ladies of the Castle.
Tuesday May 12	SHANNON	Full day tour of Ireland's most musical county. Visit the spectacular Cliffs of Moher (remember the opening scene in "Ryan's Daughter"?), the resort town of Lisdoonvarna, then slip into County Galway to see William Butler Yeats' hideaway castle, Thor Ballylee, and the classic ruins of Coole Park. Evening trip along the lovely shores of Lough Derg and stop in the famed Merriman Tavern. Dinner at Fitzpatrick's.

Wednesday
May 13
	SHANNON
	KILLARNEY
		Leave Shannon and drive south to Ireland's
		most famous locale, the Lakes of Killarney. Stop
		at Adare, a beautiful village with thatched
		cottages.
		    Arrive at the hotel in Killarney.
		        TORC GREAT SOUTHERN HOTEL

DATE	PLACE	ITINERARY 105-19 ONE PAGE NO. 2

Wednesday May 13 (cont'd)		Afternoon and evening free in Killarney for jaunting car rides around the lakes, trip to Gap of Dunloe, tour of Muckross or whatever takes your fancy. Dinner at the hotel.
Thursday May 14	KILLARNEY	You will thoroughly enjoy this swing around the Dingle Peninsula, one of Ireland's most scenic and historic spots. See ancient beehive huts, the Skellig Islands where hermit monks survived, the quaint villages of this Irish speaking area. Time for pub stops, craft shops. Stopover in Tralee for sightseeing and shopping before returning to Killarney. Dinner at the hotel. Entertainment or a talk on Irish folk and fairy tales this evening.
Friday May 15	KILLARNEY BLARNEY	Leave Killarney in the morning. Dazzling seascapes make this a scenic treat. The breath-taking views from a winding coastal road, palm trees and lush floral displays are a surprise. Pass Daniel O'Connell's birthplace and residence. Lovely Glengarriff, favorite vacation spot for De Gaulle; to mystic Gougane Barra, source of the River Lee and seat of Saint Finbarr's monastic settlement. A fresh salmon lunch at Johnny Creedon's country hotel in Inchigeela; then to Blarney for a castle tour and a chance to kiss the fabled stone. Arrive at the hotel in Blarney. <u>HOTEL BLARNEY</u> Dinner at the hotel.
Saturday May 16	BLARNEY CORK WATERFORD	Leave Blarney and drive to Cork for a visit of Ireland's second largest city, with its fine shops, literary reputation and rebel history. Follow the coast to Waterford, with a

DATE	PLACE	ITINERARY 105-19 ONE PAGE NO. 3
Saturday May 16 (cont'd)		stop en route at the Waterford Crystal Factory. Continue to Arrive at the hotel in Waterford. HOTEL ARDREE Dinner at the hotel. Evening of traditional Irish music.
Sunday May 17	WATERFORD CASHEL GALWAY	Morning at leisure to attend church services. Leave Waterford and travel via Carrick-on-Suir, Cahir, to Cashel for a tour of the Rock of Cashel, historic site dating back to the sixth century. Travel east of Lough Derg, then to Galway with its lyrical bay and continue to Arrive at the hotel in Galway. GREAT SOUTHERN HOTEL Dinner at the hotel.
Monday May 18	GALWAY	A tour of rugged Connemara is scheduled for today. Enjoy the scenic lakes and hills and stop at Kylemore Abbey and Clifden. This is "Quiet Man" country. See Ashford Castle at Cong, Ross Abbey and other sites before returning to Galway. Dinner at the hotel. Special entertainment this evening.
Tuesday May 19	GALWAY	Full day at leisure for independent activities. Suggestions include a day-long trip to the Aran Islands, shopping, or a long walk around the Bay. See the Gladdagh, Spanish Arches, or the islands made famous by John Millington Synge. Dinner at the hotel.
Wednesday May 20	GALWAY CASTLEBAR	Leave Galway and stop at the famous Marian Shrine at Knock before continuing on to Arrive at this delightful castle-like country mansion surrounded by sixty acres of parkland for lodging. BREAFFY HOUSE HOTEL Dinner at the hotel.

DATE	PLACE	ITINERARY 105-19 ONE	PAGE NO. 4
Thursday May 21	CASTLEBAR	Drive into Yeats country via Collooney and Lake Gill. See Ben Bulben then stop at Yeats' burial place at Drumcliffe and on to spectacular Mullaghmore with Lord Mountbatten's modern castle; the seaside resort of Bundoran; Bally-Shannon and Donegal town, with Red Hugh's castle. Fish and Chips in Killybegs; the Glenties and Barnesmore Gap. A stop at Ellen's Pub, a 300-year old pub in a remote corner of Sligo. Dinner in Sligo. Return to Castlebar for overnight.
Friday May 22	CASTLEBAR DUBLIN	Leave Castlebar and drive across the green rolling Midlands to Dublin, tracing part of the Shannon; seeing the estate of the novelist, Maria Edgeworth, with probable stops at Kells, where the priceless manuscript was found, and Navan, International Headquarters of the Columban Fathers, to Arrive at the hotel in Dublin, historic capital of Ireland. HOTEL ROYAL DUBLIN Dinner at the hotel. Tickets provided for this evening's performance of "The Passing Day" at the famed Abbey Theatre.
Saturday May 23	DUBLIN	A completely free day in Dublin with time for shopping, browsing and sightseeing on your own.
Sunday May 24	DUBLIN	Free time for church service before departing on city sightseeing tour. An interesting drive through the city including views of government buildings, St. Stephen's Green and Mansion House with visits to Trinity College, Phoenix Park and the Botanic Gardens. This afternoon at leisure or take an optional tour to Glendalough. Dinner and celebrated Irish Cabaret at the Burlington Hotel.

DATE	PLACE	ITINERARY 105-19 ONE PAGE NO. 5
Monday May 25	DUBLIN NEW YORK CHICAGO OMAHA	Transfer provided from the hotel to the airport. Leave Dublin by Aer Lingus flight #105 12:00 Noon (Lunch aloft) U.S.A. Arrive New York (John F. Kennedy) 3:45 P.M. Go though U.S. Customs. Change planes. Leave New York (John F. Kennedy) by United Airlines flight #415 7:00 P.M. Arrive Chicago 8:30 P.M. Change planes. Leave Chicago by United Airlines flight #667 9:35 P.M. (Dinner aloft) Arrive Omaha 10:52 P.M. * * * *

STATEMENT OF CONDITIONS/GROUP TOURS

WHAT THE RATE INCLUDES: **Date:** 4/15/81   **Ref.#** 105-19 ONE ypg

The services and arrangements specified,
commencing in: Shannon, IRELAND   on: May 11, 1981

and terminating in: Dublin, IRELAND   on: May 25, 1981

TRANSPORTATION: (seat reservations on trains included where possible)
(A) Private motorcoach, including all running and garaging expenses, taxes, tolls, driver's maintenance and ferry charges.

(B) Rail transportation   -----------

(C) Sleeping car reservation   -----------

(D) Local ship transportation   -----------

(E) Other transportation   -----------

HOTELS: Subject to confirmation of the hotels specified in the itinerary, or similar:
    Twin bedded rooms with private bath, single rooms at supplementary charge.

MEALS:
    Continental Breakfast: ---------

    Full Irish breakfast included

    Table D'Hote Luncheons: -------------

    Table D'Hote Dinners: included except for May 23

    Meals en route, meals while on excursions away from hotels and special meals as shown in the itinerary are included.
    lunch on May 15
TIPS AND TAXES:
Service charges and local taxes as imposed by hotels and local governments are included.

TRANSFERS:
From and to airports, rail stations, steamship piers and inter-city motorcoach terminals by private motorcoach.

LUGGAGE: 1   average size suitcase(s) (29" x 19" x 9") will be carried free of charge. A small overnight bag may
also be taken but this is at the expense and responsibility of the owner at all times. Luggage is at owner's risk throughout
the tour and should be insured.

SIGHTSEEING: As listed in the itinerary, includes transportation, services of guides, and entrance fees when accompanied by a guide.

SPECIAL SERVICES: Knappogue Banquet May 11, Abbey Theatre tickets
May 22, Irish Cabaret May 24. (Other entertainments arranged
personally by Mr. Reilly).

TOUR CONDUCTOR: The services of a professional courier will be provided from   -----------

PRICE OF TRIP: All rates quoted are based on the present value of foreign currencies in relation to the United States
Dollar and on tariffs now in effect, and are subject to confirmation and adjustment when final payment is made. The price
includes preparation and processing of the itinerary.

NOT INCLUDED: AIR TICKETS (unless especially indicated) airport taxes, after lunch or dinner coffee or tea, bever-
ages, items of personal nature such as laundry, tips on shipboard, etc.

Page 2

STATEMENT OF CONDITIONS (CONTINUED)

ARRANGEMENTS and SERVICES NOT INCLUDED in TOURS

All items not shown as included. Cost of passport, visas, wines, liquors, mineral waters, after lunch and dinner coffee, tea, milk, etc., laundry, valet service, a la carte meals, excess luggage, personal tipping and tipping for arrangements and services not included in tour arrangements, also theatre tickets, landing and embarkation taxes at airports and seaports, unless stated as being included, deck chairs, rugs, Transatlantic, Transpacific, etc., fares (Sea or Air) and other air or sea transportation not shown as being included. Baggage and personal insurance which is recommended.

GENERAL RESPONSIBILITY

Our Company and/or Allied Travel Inc., acts only as agent for the hotels, steamship companies, railroads, airlines, or owners or contractors providing accommodations, transportation or other services, and all coupons, exchange orders, receipts, contracts and tickets are issued subject to any and all tariffs, terms, and conditions under which any accommodations, transportation or any other services whatsoever are provided by such hotels, steamship companies, railroads, airlines or owners or contractors, and issuance and acceptance of any such coupons, exchange orders, receipts, contracts and tickets shall be deemed to be consent of the further conditions:

(a) That neither Our Company and/or Allied Travel Inc., nor any of its affiliated or subsidiary companies shall be or become liable or responsible for any loss, injury or damage to person, property or otherwise in connection with any accommodations, transportation or other services resulting, directly or indirectly, from acts of God, dangers incident to the sea, fire, breakdown in machinery or equipment, acts of governments or other authorities, de jure or de factor, wars, whether declared on not, hostilities, civil disturbances, strikes, riots, thefts, pilferage, epidemics, quarantines, customs regulations, delays or cancellations of or changes in itinerary or schedules, or from any causes beyond the control of Our Company and/or Allied Travel Inc., for any loss or damage resulting from improper or insufficient passports, visas, or other documents, and that neither Our Company *and/*or Allied Travel Inc., nor any of its affiliated or subsidiary companies shall be or become liable or responsible for any additional expense or liability sustained or incurred by the Purchaser as a result of any of the foregoing causes; and

(b) That the coupons, exchange orders, tickets and/or contracts in use by any hotels, steamship company, railroad, airlines, owner or contractor providing accommodations, transportation or other services shall constitute the sole contract between such hotel, steamship company, railroad, airlines, owner or contractor and the Purchaser of the tickets and/or the ticket holder.

Our Company and/or Allied Travel Inc., reserve the right in its sole discretion, to make such alteration in the itinerary as it may deem necessary or desirable and to decline to accept or retain any person as a member of any tour at any time in which event no refund will be made for any part of a tour not taken or for any accommodation or services not used.

A member may leave or abandon his or her trip at any time but at the members sole risk, cost and expense and without any refund or allowances for the period of absence of for any unearned or unused portion of the tour of facility subsequent to such abandonment unless specifically provided for and mutually agreed.

PRICE OF TOUR: All rates quoted are based on the value of foreign currencies in relation to the United States dollar and on tariffs in effect on the date shown on Page 1 "Date Prepared", and are subject to adjustment either way when the final payment is made. All rates quoted are accepted by all party's concerned and include all charges for handling and operation.

3

The Tour Manager

"Tour managers make or break a tour." That's the opinion of one West Coast agent. Another adds that "even a bad tour can be fun with the right person as escort." A less sanguine view was expressed by a Midwestern travel agency manager, who declared: "Only five per cent of the people who conduct tours are worth a damn!"

These comments underline the importance of the person in charge of the tour—the manager, escort, host, or leader. In the past, agencies were fairly careless about the caliber of individuals they dispatched as escorts, but they are now more conscious of their responsibilities to paying customers. They strive to get the best people, showing a greater concern and selectivity.

What Is a Tour Manager?

Regardless of the title you bestow on this person, the duties are somewhat consistent. They amount to overseeing the group of tourists, making certain that their expectations are realized to the fullest potential.

There are *professional tour leaders,* men and women who make their living, or a significant part of it, from escorting travelers. Often they are based in destination countries and work familiar territory year after year. While this occupation offers an excellent opportunity to travel and to meet new people, it's not as glamorous as it looks or sounds. For one thing, it's hard work; for another, the pay is nothing to get excited about. There is also the chance of disagreeable passengers, hitches in the itinerary, boredom with the routine, and the impediments such a lifestyle places on relationships. A high percentage of the full-time tour leaders are single.

Pros are usually tied in with specific tour operators. They are often multilingual and conversant with the customs and culture of their specialty areas. They receive individualized training for the job, frequently serve an apprenticeship, and periodically attend refresher courses. They may also possess a disproportionate share of the traits covered later in this chapter.

Freelance escorts may serve a number of companies and their commitment may be as complete as the fulltime leaders', or as short as they can afford to make it. Free-lancing is less secure, but does allow for a certain amount of freedom and variety, plus the possibility of negotiating terms. The freelancer may be every bit as educated and knowledgeable as the fulltime professional, and usually has some language skills.

Then there is the *occasional tour escort,* the person who takes a trip or two a year, the individual for whom this book will be most valuable. Their duties could be more organizational and managerial, and less informative. They may not have a second language or the complete command of alien geography and culture. Perhaps their host duties will be supplemented by the commentary of a local or regional guide.

The occasional escort may be a member of a travel agency staff. Some like this duty—but not too often. Old timers get quite expert, and their trips fill up regardless of the destination. Tourists know they'll be taken care of, and that they'll have fun.

Non-travel-agency people may also escort. Their interests, expertise, or visibility may lead them to this undertaking. The trip may be their annual or semi-annual vacation or, if they have considerable free time, it may be an adjunct to their regular travel.

Duties Of the Tour Manager

There is no set roster of duties for the tour manager, although some responsibilities are fairly common. It depends somewhat on the individuals involved and the tasks which must be performed. The more things a leader is able to do, the more valuable this person becomes, regardless of the number of support personnel involved.

Generally, the tour manager (or leader or host or escort—the words are often used interchangeably) must see that the conditions of the tour, as spelled out in the published itinerary, are fulfilled, and that the individual travelers are satisfied with the arrangements. This means handling emergencies as well as routine chores. The manager is something like a scoutmaster or platoon leader or office supervisor. He or she is in charge in virtually every important way.

Depending on talent and experience, the manager may also assume some or all of the local guide duties. If he or she knows the country, commentary may be shared with a local person or handled completely. A theatre tour to New York, escorted by the director of a community playhouse or a college drama instructor, may not require another local guide—unless tourists want a city tour. Weekend football excursions would not normally add personnel for travelogue remarks. A cruise usually eliminates the need for more than an escort.

Even when the tour includes an experienced local guide, it helps if the escort can share some microphone time. Passengers expect a certain amount of this, and it also frees up the professional guides somewhat. Exchanging comments, stories, jokes, and songs makes for a pleasant combination.

Prior to embarking, the manager may also be active in helping to publicize the tour.

Where Do Tour Leaders Come From?

Excluding the professional or freelancer, occasional leaders may come from the ranks of educators, religious leaders, entertainment figures, political personalities, retired military personnel, individuals in business or the professions, and others.

Teachers may take a study group to a foreign country, or build a package around their specialty, or may merely use their group skills and blocks of free time to see new landscapes. Ministers are featured as leaders for tours to the Holy Land or European shrines. Entertainers, including local radio and TV personalities, have their adherents and may promise a good time. Incumbent politicians, like a state governor, offer tourists a little prestige. Farmers may lead other farmers, doctors may escort their colleagues, and ski fanatics may gather those with similar persuasions.

Are Men or Women Better Tour Leaders?

John Baccanello, director of recruitment and training for Cosmos, declared in a *Travel Weekly* article (2/19/81) that women are superior, citing their stamina, openness, fairness, handling of people, and reactions in emergencies as a notch ahead of their male counterparts. Seventy-five per cent of Cosmos tour escorts are women. That, of course, is one agency's opinion. Since tour escorting on a full-time basis is somewhat seasonal, men may be less likely to apply but, even so, only about six per cent of those who apply to Cosmos for escort duties are hired.

Those who favor male tour escorts point to predominantly female passenger lists, serious crises like war and insurrection, and the presumed father-figure role. One woman travel agency head claims that "women sometimes act badly around female escorts."

On balance, sex doesn't seem to enter too much into the characterization of good or bad escorts; there are some of each in both genders.

Qualifications and Qualities Of a Tour Manager

Some tour managers are specifically trained for this role; most are not. The majority of leaders must make do with a few sheets of written suggestions, their own common sense, and whatever experience they have accumulated. Consequently, in selecting someone to lead a tour, some general and personal attributes should be checked out.

SKILLS, ASSETS, AND TALENTS

Despite our constitutional guarantee, all men (and women) are not created equal. Some are brighter than others; some have better health; some are gifted with more varied backgrounds. What you want in a tour leader is a mix of as many strengths as possible, along with a minimum of weaknesses. Some of these assets are learned, while others are inherent. Of the acquired assets, these few might be mentioned:

- *The ability to attract prospects* The tour manager should be a positive sales factor, because of personality, known managerial ability, or prestige. Some travelers want a status symbol; others want security; still others seek the promise of a good time. The person who will lead the group should be able to command a following.

- *Knowledge of the area* Everyone has to start fresh somewhere, but having been there before is a definite asset, enabling the tour escort to speak with more authority, to counsel wisely on facilities and attractions, to judge the length of travel days, and to recognize possible problems. This sort of person figures out ways to avoid crowds at Windsor Castle and the Vatican, and knows the reputation of restaurants in Suva.

- *A grasp of the destination language* Such skills are required of the professional, but most occasional leaders would be without conversational speech. They end up in places where they must rely totally on the local guide. Nevertheless, if a working knowledge of the language is part of the tools of even the amateur leader, that's a plus—particularly in places like Russia and China. Not only the more common languages, like French, German and Italian, may be helpful but also, in certain circumstances, a fundamental grasp of sign language.

- *Education and intelligence* Although these two attributes should coincide, they may not. Some educated individuals are not models of intelligence, and many intelligent people may not have much formal education beyond high school. Still, you want someone as a leader who is bright, who is quick to absorb and retain information, who speaks well, and who has somehow acquired good taste and good manners. The leader, however, should not be an intellectual who overpowers or bores the traveler. The best escorts are those who are only slightly smarter (but a lot more experienced) than the people they serve.

- *Experience and age* Again, these factors should coalesce, but sometimes they don't. Some elders never seem to learn from experience, and some youngsters seem born mature. Age isn't everything, but a few gray hairs help in commanding attention and respect. However, it's better to have a competent youngster than an incompetent veteran. While direct travel experience is best, other experiences in leadership roles may transfer. The trick is to mold this alternate background in tourist terms. A financial tycoon, used to ordering his minions around, might produce a profitable balance sheet but he'd make a poor escort.

- *First aid skills* As we'll see later, the leader must be cautious about assuming any medical burdens. But skills like artificial respiration, CPR, water safety, and first echelon first aid are valuable leadership adjuncts. Having someone competent in these areas provides a lot of comfort to tourists.

- *A penchant for details* Organizational skills are often undervalued, particularly in areas like tour leadership where the emphasis is on charisma. You still want someone who thinks ahead, looks ahead, and calls ahead; someone who plots the itinerary in advance and monitors it daily; someone who is able to keep clear, complete, and accurate records. Leaders who slough off these duties are the curse of tour operators and agency managers. The good tour manager is always alert, always calculating, and always making notes.

PERSONALITY TRAITS

When you list desirable traits in any job description, you invariably create a perfect specimen. No human being measures up to these models. There are gaps in all our psyches. Still, this occupational litany sets forth characteristics one would hope to find in an employee, including the demanding role of tour escort. Given below are the assets most often mentioned in a survey of tour leaders or operators,

- *Forcefulness, decisiveness* Regardless of other qualities, the leader has to be able to lead, has to have the ability to manage people, has to be able to make a decision. This is no job for an uncertain, timid personality.

- *A positive outlook* The tour leader is an optimist, at least externally. And this optimism must be made contagious. Negative or cynical leaders are a drag. While rose-colored glasses shouldn't be in the leader's carry-on bag, a certain maturity is essential, enabling him or her to maintain a perspective and to communicate this confidence.

- *Tact* Escorts must be diplomats, both with their tour members and with the suppliers of services. Gossip must be ignored; confidences have to be honored; feelings must be considered. Tour leadership can be exhausting and exasperating, but the tour leader must remain above the petty elements. He or she deals with each situation as firmly and pleasantly as possible.

- *Honesty and loyalty* These virtues must be practiced on behalf of the escort's own integrity, the people he or she is leading, and the company that is paying the bills. Everything must be above board. There should be no hidden expenses, no cheating of clients. The leader shouldn't knock the firm for which he or she works. This is both unfair and unwise, and ultimately reflects back on the escort. In crises, the tour manager levels with passengers and employers. And reports and expenses are scrupulously handled.

- *Assertiveness* This term has become a buzzword in today's society, and thousands of individuals pay high fees to gain this sort of presence. The tour leader had better possess self-assurance, self-pride, and a certain amount of ego. When a desk clerk insists there are no single rooms as promised by the vouchers, the leader must be adamant. "Get me a supervisor." This doesn't mean being loud and abusive, or acting tough; it means exhibiting inner strength and resolution. It means insisting on the rights of your tour members.

- *A calm demeanor* Sweaty palms, maybe, but always a reassuring smile. The best leaders don't panic, even internally. They are cool in crises and respond immediately to emergencies. They are able to think clearly when chaos threatens. They seem at ease in the midst of trouble, and this soothes their charges. Experience helps in developing this trait, but some individuals possess it instinctively.

- *A warm personality* The previous qualities seem almost militaristic in their application. And there must be a bit of the commanding officer in the tour escort. The difference is that this is a group of independent revelers and not a platoon. The tour leader, while establishing leadership credentials, must still communicate a sunny disposition, flash that ready smile, and reveal an enthusiastic bonhomie. Tourists expect their escorts to be lively, gifted with attractive voices, and to have that essential sense of humor. It doesn't pay to be officious, cold, or imperious with tourists or with hotel and restaurant personnel. Your reputation spreads, and you may be traveling this way again.

- *A clean and neat appearance* Tour members can afford to look casual or disheveled, but the tour manager presents a perpetually scrubbed appearance. Travelers wonder how the hell he or she can keep looking so fresh. Neatness adds to authority and it sets an example for others. An unkept escort reflects poorly on himself or herself, on the sponsoring company, and on the caliber of the tour.

- *Good health* Not every tour manager has to be a dawn jogger or an isometrics fanatic, but each one should be in reasonably good health, free from debilitating complaints, and blessed with a reserve of stamina. The leader must always be "up" and stay ahead of his or her passengers. First up and sometimes the last to bed. Even when the escort is not feeling in top form, the illusion of vitality has to be there. There must also be resiliency, an ability to bounce back from the head cold or upset stomach, along with the will power to persevere, though ailing. Escorts, like mothers, can't really afford to get sick.

- *Sensitivity* In addition to plotting routes and meeting emergencies, the tour leader studies his or her passengers, anticipating personality conflicts, massaging egos, tuning in on complaints, assessing the degree of fatigue, comforting the frightened or the lonely. The escort also notices things— the new hairdo, the special dress, the newly purchased sweater, the treasured souvenir. The leader has to be part psychologist, alert to people and their moods. At the same time, the tour manager can't be too sensitive personally. The occasional griper can't get under the leader's skin. He or she must ride with the punches.

- *Flexibility* Some people panic when their routine is threatened. This often occurs with solid planners, who like things neat and orderly. The old Murphy's Law certainly applies to tours: "If anything can go wrong, it will." Planning minimizes catastrophe, but some changes are inevitable. There are equipment breakdowns, failures in communication, disagreeable and troublesome passengers, illnesses, natural disasters, transportation delays, and so on. Tour leaders think on their feet. They have the ability to change directions when the situation dictates.

- *Diligence* Some tour leaders coast. They sit out the cruise alone. They get their people to a destination and disappear. Perhaps they are holed up with local buddies or merely incommunicado in their own rooms. They do a minimum of work. The real leader isn't afraid of hard work. He or she is on top of things, handling any reasonable task that needs to be done. This sort of escort is interested in everything working well, including making sure that each tourist enjoys his or her free time.

- *Sacrifice* As with any leadership role, the escort must be willing to forego his or her own comfort for the good of the traveler. This may mean a swap of accommodations, or the interruption of some personal plan. The leader must be willing to eat last, drink last, relax last. This attitude persists from takeoff until the last bags leave the Stateside carousel.

- *Anticipation* While flexibility is a necessary virtue, the wise escort figures out in advance everything that might go wrong and tries to insure against these occurrences. This means frequent conversations with the bus driver or cruise personnel, advance phone calls, a survey of facilities before leading in the group. Nothing is taken for granted; all items are checked and rechecked.

- *Ability to create lasting friendships* An experienced escort is able to bring people together, to seek out the lonely and integrate them, to make quartets of couples. The diverse group of individuals is made to think like a family, like men and women who enjoy each other and who want a minimum of friction. At the end of a good tour, the members are almost unwilling to part. They frequently stay in touch with each other and often travel together on subsequent trips.

NEGATIVE QUALITIES

Nobody has all the good qualities listed above, at least not in perfection. Every tour leader is partially flawed. What tour operators want to avoid, however, are those potential leaders who are cursed with major defects. You don't want escorts who are dishonest, who are chronic drunks, whose lechery is infamous, who are congenitally lazy, whose manner is abrasive, who are frightened and unstable, who have no talent for managing others. These qualities are a liability in any job, but they spell disaster if inflicted on a group of people living in close proximity for weeks.

Compensation

As mentioned earlier, escorting tours is not a highly paid profession. The rewards are more psychic—the love of travel, the chance for expense-paid amusement, the desire to share one's knowledge with others. While these inducements are present, the job remains hard work, and will never be adequately compensated.

The escort may draw an annual or seasonal salary, may receive a stipend for each trip, or may take the tour for expenses. His or her hotel, food, and regular entertainment will be paid, and there should be a fund in the leader's possession for phone calls, buying occasional drinks for tour members, supplying an occasional modest surprise, for tipping and for emergencies. If the escort is unsalaried, and if the tour makes money, many operators will share some of this largesse with the leader, particularly if this person helped with promotion and recruitment. This seems only fair.

The tour escort never solicits tips from passengers. If the subject arises, he or she should opt out of the conversation. Advice may be given, if requested, on gratuities to drivers, local guides, and others, but the leader should be indifferent to personal tips. If the tour members take up a collection for the escort, this may be accepted, but it's a good idea to blunt such fund-raising in advance. Many times a tour group will buy a gift for the leader and this may be acknowledged, particularly if it would be awkward to refuse. *But, to repeat, the escort should do nothing to encourage such gifts, especially those of a monetary nature.*

Authority Of the Tour Leader

A tour leader's lines of authority aren't absolute, but they are substantial. Most tour operators spell them out in their manuals. In general, the escort is expected to maintain discipline and to meet emergencies with resonsibility. This means the tour leader may dismiss from the tour individuals who are making others uncomfortable or who are making the leader's job impossible. The escort may also suggest itinerary changes for the convenience or safety of passengers, and he or she may allocate portions of the emergency fund when reason dictates. The leader is in charge and calls the shots.

Even within the broad responsibility, the leader has to be aware that such jurisdiction is limited. Nothing should be done that will later provoke unnecessary criticism of the escort or the company, or that may result in a lawsuit, or the witholding of payment by a supplier. Thoughtless personal attacks, unwarranted accusations, unauthorized medical advice, poor solutions in time of danger, reckless disregard for the published itinerary, arbitrary handling of personal conflicts—these and other lapses make both the leader and the operator vulnerable.

The escort should not demand alterations in the programmed itinerary. Such changes may be requested if the escort feels tour members are tired or would be otherwise inconvenienced, but this should be handled carefully.

The best course is a blend of diplomacy with authority. Perform those duties you have an obligation to perform, but keep all things in perspective.

Tour leadership is not democratic, but neither is it autocratic. It revolves around good judgment and common sense. You lead, but you never seem to dictate. Leaders should review their responsibilities with their employers so there can be no misunderstandings. Many companies have their own guidelines, regulations, and limitations, in addition to the general terms governing group leadership.

Training

Nothing beats experience, but experience takes time. Fortunately, there are some resources available to beginners.

Company manuals are useful tools. They can be brief folders capsulizing primary escort duties, or detailed brochures covering everything from lost passport to typical gratuities. Conversations with experienced escorts are another possibility. In these discussions, the newcomer should take notes and should have a list of questions to be answered. If the veteran has been to the specific locale the beginner plans to visit, so much the better.

COURSES AND ORGANIZATIONS

There are travel schools which include sessions on tour escorting, and college curricula which also touch on this specialty. The School of Continuing Education of New York University offers a complete course in tour managing and guiding. Its initial aim is to provide competent tour escorts for visitors to America, inculcating all of the skills found in the best of foreign escorts. This six-week course is intended for individuals who are at least 21 years of age, who have a college background, and who plan on a career in tour management. A second language is desirable but optional.

This course is the brainchild of the International Association of Tour Managers, a professional organization of some 1,200 members in 38 regions around the world. Begun in 1961 in London to upgrade and standardize tour management, the association defines its objectives as "the maintenance of an accepted code of conduct amongst professional Tour Managers, thereby enlisting the confidence of the travel trade and public." Not a union but an association, IATM screens all membership applications carefully, requiring five years of tour management experience, references from members and employers, personal interviews, and confidential general membership approval. Members wear a small oval gold badge and meet annually in different international locations. Allied memberships are allocated to tourism-related firms and individuals, such as hotels, restaurants, carriers, travel agents, shopping centers, entertainment centers, and other organizations.

IATM officers point out that tourists to the United States now outnumber those from the United States and emphasize that there are not enough experienced tour managers to handle this influx. They stress the importance of the tour manager as an ambassador who can soften cultural shock for visitors to our shores. For information on IATM membership, or on the NYU six-week course, interested persons should write to International Association of Tour Managers, North American Region, 100 Bank Street, Suite 3J, New York, New York 10014.

Other travel organizations (ASTA, ARTA, ICTA) periodically offer programs that deal with tour management, and some helpful books and periodicals are available.

4

Preparing For the Tour

The more you prepare, the less likelihood of something going wrong, or of something being left behind. Tour members (aided, perhaps, by the agency), have to get their acts together, and so do tour operators, travel agencies, and tour managers. Checklists are essential. Too many items are involved to trust to memory. Well in advance of the hectic final days before a trip, the tour escort should have a complete roster of things to be accomplished, and should tick these off as completed. A few of these chores take minutes; others take weeks.

Gathering Further Information

Even though some tour managers merely accompany the group, looking after routine details, it always helps to have some knowledge of the places to be visited. Tourists expect this. They'll ask questions about monetary exchange, or good restaurants, or prominent landmarks, or distances. They may query you on flora and fauna and history. "What is that yellow bush we keep seeing?" "How many francs in a dollar?" "Where's a good place to get fish?" While the local guide may field many of these, it increases the stature of the tour manager if some useful responses are made.

If this is a regular beat for the manager, the problem is largely solved, although it helps to keep current and to review new material. For those unfamiliar with the destination, various educational aids exist. They help the leader first to learn, and then to learn to share.

As a first priority, the escort must become familiar with maps of the countries to be visited. Get good maps—detailed maps—not sketchy ones that show only major cities. Travel the entire trip mentally, considering distance and terrain, familiarizing yourself with place-names and key highways. Refer to the map when studying the itinerary or perusing guide books. City maps are also helpful, particularly for places like London, Paris, Rome, Tokyo, New York, and other major population centers.

Most libraries are well stocked with guide books. Fodor and Fielding are the big names, but there are Blue Guides, Mobil Guides and dozens of others. In these pages the escort will find information on mileage, day tours, famous landmarks, history, culture, hotels and restaurants, even average temperatures, clothing recommendations, and foreign phrases. Details on the areas to be visited should be studied closely and committed to memory, if possible. Most guides are very portable and can be carried on tour for instant reference.

In addition to tour guides there are many travel books that provide a more relaxed look at these nations, often including helpful photos and interesting anecdotes. Depending on how deeply the escort plans to get into the subject, volumes on history, art, sociology, and anthropology may also prove useful.

The United States Passport Service prepares material on most foreign countries. While its prose is terse, each brochure does focus on specific items of concern to traveling Americans. Consulates are also rich sources of information, as are the tourist bureaus in most countries. From the latter, you get not only maps and the typical brochures, but also regional booklets, schedules of events for the year, and items as specific as subway and train timetables.

The International Association of Tour Managers provides courses and a newsletter. ARTA and ICTA offer both seminars and printed materials, including, from ICTA, such recent publications as *Marketing Travel to Music Groups,* by William Wardell and *Travel and Stay Healthy,* by Joan Ehrenfeld. Eric Olson, a tour manager in Hollywood, publishes a magazine called *The Tourmaker.* The International Travel Library publishes a series of books covering hotels and resorts, international steamship schedules, a *World Travel Directory,* a *Travel Market Yearbook* and other volumes. From the Brigham Young University Language and Intercultural Research Center come "Culturgrams" at 25¢ each (less in volume). These are four-page pamphlets capsulizing the history, customs, lifestyles, and language of sixty-nine different countries. *Traveling Times,* another California-based tabloid, carries articles of a general and professional nature.

Then there are consumer publications like *Travel/Holiday, Travel Leisure,* and trade journals like *Travel Weekly, Travel Agent,* and *Travel Trade.* Many other magazines carry travel details, as do local and national newspapers. The escort should keep files of clippings from these sources on destinations he or she is likely to visit.

Familiarization tours are obviously another great asset, and so are conversations with persons who have traveled to that destination or, perhaps, lived there. The escort should pick their brains, taking as many notes as possible. Many travel agencies require their traveling personnel to file detailed reports, which are then made available to other consultants and tour managers.

Agency manuals must also be learned by tour managers and, if this is their first time as escorts, they should sit down with a veteran and bone up on the pitfalls.

Some fundamental knowledge of the language is a big plus. Short of being proficient in the native tongue, the escort may still take a crash course in a language, or cram with a self-teaching record or book. Knowing how to read common signs, menu notations, and hotel information is very helpful, and even the stylized phrases for standard conversations can assist one out of a difficult spot. Besides its emergency value, this basic language skill is a good way to establish group authority.

Finally, the escort should certainly be aware of major local customs, particularly the taboos, and of the rate of monetary exchange.

The Itinerary

Tour managers must mentally tour the entire route before the trip takes off. Think through possible hitches. If you drive from Kendal to Stratford, will you have time for supper before the Shakesperian performance? Does the excursion boat to the islands leave on a Tuesday? Are the shops open on the Monday afternoon you've scheduled for shopping? Can you reach the crystal factory before it closes for the day? Have you allowed enough time at the pyramids? Should you book a big banquet the night of your arrival?

The agency will normally work out the hotels with the tour operator, but the experienced tour escort is also consulted on these, or should be. While the *Official Hotel and Resort Guide* does an excellent job, as do some of the other reputable guide books, there is no substitute for having been on the premises or having talked with someone who has stayed there. You discover that the hotel is lovely but has no porters. Or you're advised not to book rooms on the side next to the subway. Or you find that there is a new and an old section. Or you learn the hotel is perfect except for location, which is eight miles from town. There may be no good restaurant nearby, or the air-conditioning is balky, or the bathrooms limited. Perhaps the place has changed hands and has been remodeled. Maybe it is dangerously short of staff. Since the tour manager will have to live with any complaints, good hotel selection concerns him or her.

All planned events should be nailed down. Perhaps you intend to have a chamber music recital at the hotel. The group and hotel have both responded affirmatively, but somehow the interaction between both never comes off. Don't assume that anything will go right automatically. Check these details out. If you are attending the medieval banquet, are you making the first or second sitting? Does the cruise ship have the amenities you've promised clients? What's playing at the Palladium?

Seat assignments on airplanes and cabin assignments on ships should be known. Cruise ships supply stateroom charts, and there are diagrams of the different aircraft configurations. Tourists will want to know these things, so having the details in advance is an advantage.

Organize Commentary Materials

Assuming the escort is going to have something to say, even if he or she isn't doing the bulk of the descriptive work on the tour, it pays to gather material well in advance of the trip, and to collect it in some readily usable form.

A three-ring notebook with flexible binder works well. Two or three of these fit handily into any luggage. Perhaps one contains the itinerary, addresses of foreign contacts, national and city maps, maps of the underground systems, charts on monetary exchange, names of restaurants, list of optional tour choices, facts about entertainment selections, hotel rooming lists, mail information, several passenger lists, pages from the agency's tour manual, tipping suggestions, and other items directly pertinent to the trip.

The second (and third) book can be filled with historical and cultural facts, jokes and anecdotes, songs, appropriate poetic and literary selections, and other materials. The first notebook helps the escort accomplish the required duties, while the second or third gives this person something to say en route.

The First Notebook

Here, in more detail, are some of the items to be found in the working notebook.

- *Passenger list* The basic list gives the traveler's name and address, plus the first name of the spouse. The escort must get to know this list thoroughly, along with the preferred method of addressing each passenger. To this fundamental information might be added: passport number; notes on general health; allergies, if any; special diet, birthdays and anniversaries; next of kin; people to be notified in case of problems; blood type; physician's name and address; any other helpful details.

- *Rooming lists* The roster of names can also be used for a rooming list. Merely type the name of each hotel on separate passenger list sheets. As you get to the hotels you can write the appropriate rooms by each name. You can also make special sheets for each hotel if you wish. In either case, take some extra sheets along in case you mess one up.

- *Baggage lists* A few sheets for the listing of baggage should suffice for most trips. Again the roster of names appears, with a space beside each name to record the number of bags. The bags are noted at departure time and modified if tour members add or subtract from their initial count.

- *List of persons at destination stops* You'll want the names of people in gateway cities, airline or cruise personnel, names of the tour operator contacts, motor coach company personnel, individuals in charge of special events, tourist bureau contacts, overseas representatives of your company, embassy staffs, perhaps even physicians, hotel managers, business representatives for some incentive tours, and the like. Each name should be accompanied by a title, address, and most importantly, a phone number. The more phone numbers, the better. If a telex number is desirable, add this. Try to consider all the individuals and types of individuals who would be useful in an emergency, and jot these names down.

- *Hotel confirmations* Bind into this folder all hotel confirmations, letters from hotel managers, and confirmations from restaurants, theatres, or other suppliers en route. In case of discrepancies or disputes, you have the documents with you. Include, also, all travel arrangements.

- *Detailed itinerary* This is particularly important for bus trips and less so for cruises and train tours, where stops are less frequent and scenic attractions fewer. The basic itinerary supplied by the tour operator is a start, but the escort should have an hour-by-hour docket, much more complete than the itinerary handed to tour members. This is a good place to make marginal notes about people to see or calls that should be made ahead.

- *Report forms* The escort needs space to record daily happenings— problems with passengers, missed connections, altered itinerary, hotel and restaurant assessments, and other matters. In addition, there should be an expense sheet for the recording of all monies expended by the tour manager. Since there is often little time for record keeping on tour, the more accessible and efficient these forms are, the easier the escort's task.

- *Trip brochures* A few copies of the tour brochure should be kept. The escort may need to check this en route, or the local guide or driver may want one, or suppliers may ask for a copy. Tour members may lose theirs and ask for another, and you sometimes recruit people on other, less satisfactory, tours by supplying them with a copy. Next time they may book with you.

* *Miscellaneous* Many tour managers keep extra copies of everything, from passenger lists to itineraries. They also bind in maps and informative articles, along with fact sheets, addresses of friends, and checklists of other things to do.

Pleasant Prospect Tours   France, Germany, Italy   May 1982

B A G G A G E   C O U N T

NAME	JOIN IN	NO. OF PIECES	WEIGHT
Mr. and Mrs. Burroughs	CHI	3	81#
Mrs. Elizabeth Collins	CHI	2	38#
Mr. and Mrs. Douglas	CHI	2	70#
Mr. and Mrs. Geohner	CHI	3	96# ✓
Ms. Phyllis Holly	NY	2	40#
Mr. and Mrs. Kincaid	CHI	3	74#
Mr. Arthur Paul	CHI	1	31#
Mr. and Mrs. Pifer	CHI	2	69#
Mr. and Mrs. Rodino	NY	3	82#
Mrs. Katherine Thomas	CHI	1	30#
Mr. and Mrs. Vavrina	CHI	3	95# ✓
		25	706
			39 OK
		181 706	
		166	
		162 4	

R O O M I N G   L I S T

HOTEL: Hotel Germaine

DATES: May 11-14

Mr. and Mrs. Roger Burroughs 22
Mrs. Elizabeth Collins   19
Mr. and Mrs. Leland Douglas 23
Mr. and Mrs. Karl Goehner   24
Ms. Phyllis Holly   18
Mr. and Mrs. Sean Kincaid   30
Mr. Arthur Paul   17
Mr. and Mrs. Emil Pffer   31
Mr. and Mrs. Joseph Rodino   32
Mrs. Katherine Thomas   16
Mr. and Mrs. Donald Vavrina 34

Tom Potter (Escort)   21
Claude Poisson (Courier) 8
Ralph Conte (Driver)   7

Materials for Tour Members

Tour operators and/or travel agencies regularly supply some materials to travelers. The kind and number of these gifts vary from place to place, but the idea behind the items is to provide more comfort and interest on the trip, and to allow the tourist to stay in communication with his or her relatives. The tour manager must be able to answer queries on these items. Some of the things frequently supplied are:

- *"Baby sitter" cards* These cards or sheets contain information on how the traveler can be reached en route, giving hotels, with addresses and phone numbers and telex info, plus dates and destinations. Several of these would be supplied to each tour member.

- *Mail information* This could be part of the "baby sitter" card or a separate sheet that would include the average number of days to be allowed for mail from the United States to various parts of the world; the cost of airmail postage to these same destinations; the correct manner to address air mail envelopes; details on sending cables; and other pertinent data. The travel agency is usually listed below in case relatives seek further advice.

- *Hotel listings* All hotels are listed, together with addresses and phone numbers. These sheets, too, are for relatives and friends of the tour members.

- *Passenger list.* Each tour member should get a couple of these. This makes the group more congenial, and aids those with short memories.

- *Preliminary itinerary* The final itinerary is usually given to tour members at departure time. Prior to that, perhaps all they have is the advertising brochure. However, some agencies also supply what is clearly labelled as a preliminary itinerary, giving the traveler some idea of the proposed trip.

- *Flight bags* These are an expense item for the agency and not all travel companies supply them. Those that do generally label the bags with their name, providing both identification and advertising. These should be a distinctive color and of serviceable quality. One to a client is the custom.

- *Baggage tags* Each tour member is given at least two of these, and the tour escort takes along a dozen or more to replace lost tags. A unique color and shape help with instant identification. Many companies seem to use red and green, and when several tours are in one hotel, the sorting of the bags can get confusing. A variant shape (a kiosk, a triangle, an ellipse) helps differentiate. Old tags should be removed when the new ones are applied, and many veteran travelers also stuff a business card inside each case, in the event the bag is lost and the tag torn away.

- *Maps* Some sort of map is a nice gift. Occasionally, these maps will be premarked with the route, or the escort and/or driver may mark them at the conclusion of the journey—if the passenger approves. The tour operator or tourist board may supply these and they are usually not in great detail. Passengers should be encouraged to purchase their own more complete maps.

MAIL AND CABLE INFORMATION

The schedule below indicates the number of days required for AIRMAIL DELIVERY from various points in USA to your friends or relatives abroad

Letters TO Mailed FROM	Europe	Middle-East	Far-East	Pacific Islands Australia New Zealand	Hawaii	Central America	Latin America	Africa	Russia
East Coast	6	7	9	8	8	6	7	8	7
West Coast	7	8	8	8	5	6	7	8	9
Midwest	7	8	8	8	6	6	7	8	7
South	7	8	9	8	6	5	6	9	8

IMPORTANT: This applies to mail between key cities only (New York–Copenhagen, Chicago–Paris, or San Francisco–Tokyo, etc).

A day or two longer should be allowed for mail to smaller, off-the-beaten-path places. If you mail from a small town in the USA an additional one or two days should be added.

EXTRA TIME SHOULD BE ALLOWED FOR LETTERS TO ARRIVE AT DESTINATION PRIOR TO THE WEEKEND WHEN DEPARTURE OF ADDRESSEE IS BETWEEN SATURDAY NOON AND MONDAY NOON.

Airmail Letter Postage from the United States to:

18¢—1st ounce 17¢—Ea. Add't. ounce	35¢ per ½ oz. up to 2 ounces 30¢ Ea. Add't. ½ ounce	40¢ per ½ ounce up to 2 ounces 35¢ Ea. Additional ½ ounce
CANADA and MEXICO	CENTRAL AMERICA, COLOMBIA, VENEZUELA, THE CARIBBEAN ISLANDS, BAHAMAS, BERMUDA AND ST. PIERRE AND MIQUELON.	SOUTH AMERICA (excluding Colombia and Venezuela), EUROPE, ASIA, AFRICA, AUSTRALIA AND PACIFIC ISLANDS.

Air-letter envelopes, obtainable at any US Post Office, may be sent to any point in the world for 30¢. These are good for one page message and delivery is as fast as air-mail. NO ENCLOSURES ARE PERMITTED.

Letters should be sent in the name under which guests will be registered. Also mention date of expected arrival of addressee, exactly as indicated in sample below.

```
Sender:                                                    STAMP



                Name of Guest
                HOTEL GERMAINE
                106 Rue de la Paix
                Paris, FRANCE

HOLD FOR ARRIVAL
SCHEDULED TO ARRIVE:    May 11, 1982
```

CABLE INFORMATION

Cables should be sent to the hotels "Letter Telegram." This is comparable to a Night Letter; delivered on the morning after the telegram is dispatched in the U.S.A. If faster delivery is desired, send "Straight Cable." Use first and last name of addressee. Unless full name is preferred, sign cables with only first name. The minimum cable charge includes 21 words, counting name, address, message and signature, except that name of country does not count as a word.

For further details do not hesitate to contact your relative's or friend's Travel Agent where you can obtain all information.

PLEASANT PROSPECT TOURS
4645 Loop Drive
Chicago, Illinois 60604

Phone: (312) 955-5555

FOR CAREFREE TRAVEL CONSULT YOUR A.T.I. TRAVEL AGENT

H O T E L L I S T I N G

FOR: European Holiday Tour   REF: # 111-19
     with Tom Potter

NAME OF HOTEL	CITY & COUNTRY	PERIOD OF STAY
HOTEL GERMAINE Phone: (1) 61178	Paris FRANCE	5/11 - 5/14
HOTEL AUBERGE Phone: (92) 29366	Lyons FRANCE	5/14 - 5/15
HOTEL RIVIERA Phone: (93) 314	Nice FRANCE	5/15 - 5/16
RANDAZZI HOUSE Phone: (55) 11171	Florence ITALY	5/16 - 5/17
MARIALUNA HOTEL Phone: (6) 90073	Rome ITALY	5/17 - 5/19
DER HAUPT HAUS Phone: (89) 55425	Munich GERMANY	5/19 - 5/20
FRANKFURT HILTON Phone: (611) 33925	Frankfurt GERMANY	5/20 - 5/21
DAS KASERNE HOTEL Phone: (2) 05492	Berlin GERMANY	5/21 - 5/23

Pleasant Prospect Tours
EUROPEAN HOLIDAY TOUR
May 11-May 31
1982

TOUR MEMBERS

BURROUGHS, Mr. and Mrs. Roger (Alice)
1906 N. Colonial Drive
Westbridge,Illinois 60611

COLLINS, Mrs. Elizabeth
95 Meadow Grove Avenue
Decatur,Illinois 60193

DOUGLAS, Mr. and Mrs. Leland (Doris)
2424 Osmond Lane
Chicago,Illinois 60606

GEOHNER, Mr. and Mrs. Karl (Ruth)
991 Avenue M
East Chicago,Illinois 60707

HOLLY, Ms. Phyllis
Evinrude Apartments, # 9
2536 Congress Blvd.
Glastonbury, Connecticut 05413

KINCAID, Mr. and Mrs. Sean (Alta)
1 Davis Drive
Adams, Illinois 61101

PAUL, Arthur
1110 Ranier Circle, Apt. # 17
Tanager,Illinois 60522

PFFER, Mr. and Mrs. Emil (Greta)
11915 Wakeley Avenue
Westbridge,Illinois 60611

RODINO, Mr. and Mrs. Joseph (Angie)
4670 William and Mary Court
White Plains, New York 04505

THOMAS, Mrs. Katherine
6224 Glenvale Road
Decatur,Illinois 60193

VAVRINA, Mr. and Mrs. Donald (Mary)
104 Buffalo Street
Chicago,Illinois 60606

POTTER, Tom (Tour Manager)
PLEASANT PROSPECT TOURS
4645 Loop Drive
Chicago,Illinois 60604

Home Address:
19 Alameda Lane
Locksbey,Illinois 60951

Travel Tips

The travel agency may also pass along various tips on everything from packing and photography to insurance and foreign customs. Some of this information may be given at tour group meetings before departure, but it's helpful to the participants to have it all in writing.

PASSPORTS

Remind the travelers that *everyone* must have a passport, even children. If this reminder arrives early enough, you can give them details of what is necessary in order to obtain a passport—proof of citizenship (birth certificate, affidavit of birth, baptismal certificate, or naturalization papers), identification (like a valid driver's license with the individual's signature), two recent portrait-type photos (2" x 2", color or black and white, dull finish, front view of face). Many agencies use a special polaroid camera to take such passport photos, but most travelers go to a studio specializing in this type of shot. Vending machine pictures are *not* acceptable. The photo must be signed just as the tourist signed the passport application. The passport application, incidentally, is usually supplied by the travel agent.

Along with the items mentioned above, the passport applicant must bring to the passport agency (located in the post office in larger cities) the passport and execution fees ($10 and $5 respectively in 1982). Cash is not acceptable for this transaction. Use check, money order, traveller's check, bank draft, etc.

Passports are good for five years, and must be renewed after that, either in person, as above, or by mail—if the passport is not older than eight years. The old passport serves as proof of citizenship and identification. It should be mailed, together with two new photos (signed), the fee, and the Application for Passport by Mail form.

CAMERA

Remind tourists to check their cameras to be sure they're in good shape. If they've purchased a new camera, they should experiment with it before departure, to iron out any problems. If the camera is a foreign make, they should register it with the customs authorities before leaving, to avoid the possibility of paying duty on the camera on the return trip. This goes for any foreign-made item—watch, field glasses, radio, lenses, and the like. The traveler should carry a Certificate of Registration for each of these things taken abroad.

Film is invariably cheaper in the United States, so the tour member should get plenty before departure. Because film is really the least expensive part of photography, it's a shame to run out. Experts advise that travelers not try to take both still and movie cameras, because they become burdensome and enough time can't be devoted to either, resulting in poor pictures. They also advise taking along several lenses, and are especially high on zoom lenses, since these replace several other lenses.

Other recommendations of the pro's are: insure the equipment, and take several speeds of films, anywhere from ASA 64 to ASA 400. Flash attachments, filters, cleaning equipment and other items are good to have along.

For those who are concerned about possible x-ray damage to film at airports, a hand inspection or foil protection (available in camera shops) is suggested.

On cruises, camera bugs find they can take more equipment along, since they can leave some in the cabin rather than having to tote it everywhere. The cabin is also a smart place to keep film, since it's cooler. Outside, the camera lens should be protected.

Most travelers carry their equipment rather than pack it in their luggage, where it could get damaged. And the wise photographer brings the film home to be processed—because it costs much less.

HEALTH TIPS

The destination affects much of this information, as does the age and general health of the traveler. Some areas call for shots, everything from smallpox to typhus injections, and the United States Passport Service can supply this information—as can most travel agencies. After these vaccinations, the traveler is issued a health card which must be shown once the person returns to this country.

Tour members should bring with them any prescription medicines (like heart and blood pressure pills), an extra pair of glasses and the prescription, extra false teeth, hearing aid batteries and the like.

It is advisable to have a complete checkup before leaving the country— and this goes for the escort, too!

Travel can be tiring. People may be sitting for long periods on planes and buses, getting less oxygen, losing sleep, eating irregularly, drinking more, changing time zones. These factors affect health, and stress the fact that people should moderate their habits, get all the rest they can before the trip and, en route, carry all necessary medicines, and watch the food and drink intake.

Alcohol reaches the bloodstream faster on airplanes, because of the decrease in atmospheric pressure, and the effects of alcohol are heightened by the use of medicines like antihistamines, tranquilizers, sleeping pills and motion sickness medicine. The temptation when flying is to drink more, because of boredom or anxiety—or thirst, in the less humid air. The traveler should be cautioned to resist this temptation, to minimize his or her use of medicines, and to alternate drinking with eating.

When traveling outside the normal tourist routes, the United States Public Health Service recommends that tourists take gamma globulin shots to prevent the onset of hepatitis. They add that this process should be repeated every three months during extended stays in tropical areas or developing countries.

The United States Center for Disease Control in Atlanta, Georgia, publishes a weekly chart of countries where there have been outbreaks of quarantinable diseases. People traveling to these countries despite the warnings are usually required to sign cards indicating they are aware of this potential danger.

For the handicapped traveler, the United States Travel Service, Department of Commerce, issues a brochure of travel tips, and Chatham Square Press, New York, published a book by Louise Weiss called *Access to the World*, which also treats this subject. A number of tour groups specialize in travel for the handicapped, including Evergreen Travel Service (Lynnwood, Washington), Flying Wheel Tours (Owatonna, Minnesota), Rambling Tours (Hallandale, Florida), and Vagabond Tours for the Deaf (Margate, Florida).

MONEY

Tourists should be advised to carry only a small amount of cash, including only a small amount of foreign currency, if they bring that with them. Travelers checks are still the best and safest way to carry funds, and these can be supplemented by personal checks and credit cards, preferably the credit cards most acceptable in the destination countries. A list of travelers checks and credit cards should be carried a couple of places on the traveler's person and should also be left with someone at home. Those who should be contacted in case of loss should also be listed.

If the tour is a long one, some tourists have their local bank dispatch funds to them at certain key cities. Escorts who want to avoid lugging around too much may do the same.

Money belts are recommended as safe places to keep funds, and a shirt or breast pocket for men, and the bottom of the pocketbook for women, are the safest places for wallets.

Travel/Holiday (June, 1980) also suggested the tourist prepare a dummy wallet with expired credit cards and have this more conspicuously displayed.

You can often get a small amount of foreign currency at a local bank, in tip packs, but carrying this overseas isn't usually necessary. International airports have banks on the premises, so you can exchange currency, or cash travelers checks right away.

It helps to inform the tour members of the exchange rate and about the monetary system of the nations they'll visit. Since many of them will forget this, or will panic when faced with a transaction, it's better to have something printed up, even with illustrations of the foreign coinage and bills.

ELECTRICAL APPLIANCES

Hair dryers, traveling irons, electric razors and other appliances won't work in foreign countries without special attachments (which can be purchased in this country) and adaptor plugs. Better to leave such appliances at home, if you can. If not, then someone had better bring along the required equipment to handle the current and voltage abroad. The Franzus Company publishes a brochure on foreign electrical currents, and also sells a line of convertors and other equipment. Other brand name convertors and adaptors are also available.

PACKING

This is a chore for both escort and passengers. It pays to learn the secrets of efficient packing, both for convenience and for conformation with airline or tour regulations. If possible, it's wise to pack everything in one bag whose total weight does not exceed 44 pounds. Some tour conditions vary, permitting a couple of bags, and specifying certain linear dimensions for luggage, so travelers should be aware of these specific limitations.

When measuring luggage to stay within the total 106 inches required by some airlines, keep in mind that no single bag may exceed 62 inches (length plus width plus depth). If one bag is 58 inches, this means the second one can be no more than 48 inches in total dimensions. However, if the 44 pound weight limit applies, both bags cannot exceed this limit.

Often the airlines will ignore this weight, or they may just weigh the total baggage of a tour and not worry if it adds up to a few more pounds than would be allotted per person. But the tour manager should not promise this latitude to passengers. It's better to advise them to stay within limits. The single bag under 44 pounds remains the safest alternative. (First Class passengers are allowed 66 pounds and 124 inches total.)

Regulations regarding baggage on cruise ships, planes, and domestic buses and airlines should be checked out in advance.

Carry-on luggage, which is not normally reckoned in the weight, may include purses, camera equipment, umbrella, books, usually the flight bag and similar items which may be stored under the seat. The common dimensions for such storage is figured at 44 inches. Suit bags, which can be hung in the plane's closet, are often allowed, but not guaranteed. Hat boxes or wig boxes are checked as luggage.

Besides tagging each item, including carry-on items, many veteran travelers identify their bags for ready retrieval by using decals, colored twine, a wrap-around strap or other marking. Since much luggage is similar, this makes good sense.

ASTA (American Society of Travel Agents) provides brochures titled "Packing Tips for Her" and "Packing Tips for Him" which condense a great deal of information into a few pages. Their overall analysis of the objectives of packing are:

"To protect clothes in transit; to make them easily available when you arrive; and to make them easy to repack."

Light, durable luggage is preferred, with ample room. They should have locks that work and the tourist should retain a couple of sets of keys.

And now the contents!

Some planning must go into packing. Consider the climate and season of the destination, the customs of the country (are shorts and halter tops allowed?), and the specific activities in your itinerary. Then try to economize as much as possible on selections, making each item in the wardrobe do double duty in combination with other items. Anticipating what you'll need for each occasion and organizing your clothes around one basic color is sound advice. Plan accessories, eliminating duplications and nonessential pieces. Avoid clothing that requires special care or that can be worn only once. Polyesters, wash-and-wear outfits and other convenience clothing are the best, and mix and match outfits provide a fresh look. Knit clothes also travel well.

Clothing should be comfortable—particularly shoes. One pair of shoes for walking and another for dress should suffice. A sweater, an all-weather topcoat, permanent press shirts, a crushable hat, cocktail dress or long skirt, bathing suit, at least three sets of underwear (one for wearing, one for washing, and one in reserve), quick-drying nylons and panty hose, a couple of pairs of pajamas or nightgowns (permanent press), bathing cap, a few neckties, scarf, lightweight jacket, slacks and suits, and a minimum of jewelry. The ASTA pamphlets and many travel agency brochures contain specific lists of clothing items to pack.

Avoid carrying heavy appliances, if possible, but do take along cosmetics, medicines, soap (including a small packet of detergent), sewing kit, suntan lotion (if appropriate), toilet articles, sunglasses, travel alarm, towelettes, plastic bags, safety pins, spot remover, foot powder, shoehorn, sanitary napkins, pocket flashlight, home keys, and, perhaps, insect repellent and water purifying tablets. It's also a good idea to carry along a short rope and clothespins for bathroom drying. Some of these items—the ones that may be used en route—should be in the carry-on flight bag or tote bag. These could include toothbrush and toothpaste, razor, slippers, change of stockings, washcloth, medication and the like.

Again, minimizing the load remains the objective. Porters are no longer universal, and you may end up carrying your own bags at times. To help you cut down, picture yourself struggling through customs laden with excess baggage.

Odd-shaped items, like shoes and gloves, belong at the bottom of the suitcase, and items which can be packed flat should not be folded. Extra plastic bags, plus bags for shoes, are a good idea. Some travelers recommend shoe mittens rather than plastic bags, which can scratch the shoes.

Dresses and slacks can be layered, folding overhanging edges into each other. Put tissue paper on the inside fold of garments that might wrinkle. Level out layers of clothing to prevent shifting. Tuck socks into spare spaces. Belts should be placed, unrolled, along the sides of the cases. Underwear and pajamas should be folded lengthwise in thirds and rolled, sometimes with socks in the center. Pants and jackets are sometimes interlocked in folding, with the coat folded with sleeves back. The ASTA *Tips* even shows packing diagrams.

Don't pack things like tickets, passports, and medications. These should be with your carry-on luggage. In fact, the flight bag or tote bag should be packed with the thought in mind that you might not see your other luggage for twenty-four hours. Can you survive on what you have with you? There are other miscellaneous tips:

- Buy decent luggage to begin with.
- Allow time for packing. Don't throw things in in a hurry.
- Place liquids in plastic bottles, only two-thirds full.
- Carry plastic skirt hangers.
- Bring a collapsible bag to carry gifts you buy.
- When you get to a destination, take out your clothes and hang them up. (Maids may also press things for you, if necessary on short stays.)
- Husband and wife may divide clothes, in case one bag is lost.

SAFETY

Tourists should be reminded to cancel their home deliveries (like newspapers and milk), and to have friends or neighbors check the vacant home periodically. Local police should also be notified and given the return date. All of this should be done close to departure so that details of your absence aren't passed along, and the milkman and newsboy shouldn't be given your precise schedule.

The house should be securely locked, appliances disconnected, except for a couple of lamps which should be fitted with timers to come on at set intervals.

Pay bills in advance and ask your post office to hold your mail until further notice.

Arrangements should be made for the care of plants and pets.

Travel/Holiday (June, 1981) recommends using a business address or the address of the person's travel agent on baggage tags, so that someone at the airport can't check on houses that may not be occupied.

INSURANCE

The travel agent, or the tour leader, may mention insurance to the tour members, letting them know what is available, but it's not a good idea to push insurance. Travelers may resent this. Besides life insurance, and accident insurance, the tour member may want to consider baggage insurance and cancellation insurance. The traveler should be informed about these, but should be subjected to no hard sell.

As far as the tour leader is concerned, the company often pays his or her insurance, but the leader may also be asked to handle this individually.

Added Packing Tips for the Tour Manager

Even though the tour manager has to carry more items than most travelers, the rule about minimizing effects applies here as well. Experienced leaders soon realize they have been bringing things they never used or wore, and they discard these on subsequent trips.

The tour manager should have an accordion envelope to hold tickets and baggage stubs, plus a handy wallet-like holder for travelers checks and vouchers and other important papers. These should be kept with the leader or placed in the hotel safe.

In addition to the items suggested above for all tourists, the tour manager *may* also want to take along extra baggage tags, itineraries, and passenger lists; playing cards; bottle opener; extension cord; alarm clock; rubber bands; needle and thread; motion sickness pills, laxatives, aspirin, and other common medicines; electrician's tape; maps and guide books; scissors; paper clips; ballpoint pens; notepads; face cloth; plastic sandwich bags; perhaps a traveling iron, hair dryer and convertor; perhaps a tip pack of foreign money, or liquor, or candy, or gifts.

The tour manager has to be even more careful than other tourists to avoid packing in suitcases any items he or she will need en route. Leaders must keep in mind their responsibility to others, and pack for the tour members as well as for themselves.

Meetings with Tour Members

Pretour meetings serve a variety of purposes. They introduce people to one another, help iron out details and answer questions, establish the authority of the tour manager, whet the appetites of the passengers, and may serve to entice others to book.

The number of pretour meetings may be as few as one or as many as four or five. One or two would be the norm. The travel agency would be the likely sponsor, arranging for a place (perhaps a private home or a convenient hotel suite) and for any refreshments. There could be some simple decorations to match the theme of the trip: appropriate travel posters, maps, and artifacts, and the food, too, could have a harmonious flavor—tea and scones for Ireland and the British Isles, baklava for a Grecian cruise, fortune cookies for an excursion to China.

All those who are signed on for the tour should be invited, including those who live too far away to come. Invited along with them might be others who have expressed real interest, plus friends of the tour members who might consider joining up. At least one representative of the travel agency should be on hand, plus the tour manager, and perhaps representatives of the carrier or the tour operator. Sometimes the latter two agencies may help with meeting costs.

Name tags should be issued to all attendees and an informal atmosphere should prevail. Give people a chance to know one another. Often at these meetings tourists booking single rooms but seeking a roommate may pair up. Others may discover kinships they didn't know existed. For all of them, a certain amount of anxiety is removed.

The program should be simple. The representative of the travel agency may introduce everyone, saving the professional personnel and carrier/tour operator guests until last. This representative may cover some aspects of the tour and make some suggestions for preparations. The tour manager may then take over, or share the platform with the agency representative.

The itinerary will be reviewed and ground rules established. Any antici-pated problems, like the stricter surveillance in some countries, will be covered. Travelers should be told what to expect and what unexpected things could sometimes occur. Team members then field questions, pass out materials, and review any matters left hanging. A checklist of topics helps here. The program may also include a slide show or film. When the evening (or afternoon) is winding down, the tour manager inquires if any of the non-booked guests wishes more information or wishes to sign up.

It usually works better to have the refreshments before the meeting, so that individuals can get acquainted first, and so that the questions are handled in a more organized manner. However, it's also well to have drinks or something after the more formal session, to allow further mingling, individual questions, and the opportunity for new tour members to enlist.

These pretour meetings should be well-planned and well-executed, since they set the tone for the subsequent journey.

5

Getting Away and Getting There

Like Aristotle's formula for a well-made play, each tour must have a beginning, a middle, and an end. More attention must be paid to the middle, perhaps, but the extremities are also important.

Most tours begin in airports, even those which eventually become cruise or bus trips. Consequently, the tour manager must have an effective routine for checking people in. The tour manager and a representative of the travel agency should arrive at the local airport about two hours before departure time—and this time should be checked in advance, to avoid unnecessary waiting. The airline should provide a separate check-in area, preferably at the end of the counter, and this should be identified by a sign (provided by the travel agency or airline) identifying the check-in location for tour members.

Travel agency personnel, working with the airline staff, should handle check-in procedures. This leaves the escort free to mingle with tour members, to meet their families, and to respond to last-minute questions. The escort may also pass out materials: final itineraries, maps, baggage tags, and other items. (Some agencies have more elaborate handouts at departure time. For example, Green Carpet Tours issues an "Almanac" to each traveler, containing tips on traveling, maps, and facts on places to be visited, with room for notes.) At this time, the tour escort should also note arrivals of tour members, counting those on deck and those yet to show.

While the escort socializes and tabulates, the travel agency staff member(s) tag baggage, help the airline passenger agent process tickets, count the number of pieces of luggage forwarded by each tour member, and record the appropriate number opposite each tourist's name on the Baggage Count Sheet. This sheet, plus the ticket envelopes and boarding passes, will then be turned over to the tour manager. Sometimes identifying stickers will be issued by the travel agency. They may also be attached to baggage by the agents or tour members. Carry-on luggage should also be tagged and identified.

Once the passengers have assembled, the tour manager should make an effort to keep them together. If an airline lounge is available, that's perfect. Short of that, all tour members should be alerted as to the flight time and told to be at the departure gate (or other assembly area) at a time well in advance of departure. The tour manager should also know where everyone is, particularly if there are delays and the temptation to stray is strong. Before heading for the departure gate, the tour manager must check the coffee shops, bars, gift stores, game rooms and other airport facilities. Travel agency staff members may help with this. You can never count heads too often. Just when you think everyone is on hand, some tour member decides to buy travel insurance or a paperback, or revisit the restroom. It's much safer to follow the military routine and have the group "in formation" long before they absolutely must be there.

A word of caution about airports. Since they are crowded, and since travelers are presumed to have money, this is a ripe arena for thieves. Particularly after a person has made a purchase, the professional pickpocket may be watching to see where the wallet or coin purse is stashed. Tour leaders should warn tour members to be wary. They should also be told to guard against the pairs of thieves who work in tandem. One may deliberately drop a bill where the "mark" will find it and place it in his wallet. Then the other man moves in and lifts the wallet. Being conscious of these possibilities is a prime safeguard—there is no need to spoil a vacation before it starts.

In addition to materials, like the notebooks, that the tour manager has prepared in advance, he or she now assumes responsibility for the tickets and baggage receipts. Some tour operators suggest returning these to each passenger, making them responsible, but it works more smoothly if the tour manager never lets these items out of sight.

Then the tour members get boarding passes. It's not possible to please everyone with seating, but the leader should make certain smokers and nonsmokers are properly sectionalized, and that spouses and others traveling together get adjacent accommodations. The airline's passenger agent will also help group tour members so they're not scattered all over the plane. This makes it easier for the tour manager to keep things under control.

Veteran travelers are familiar with the configuration of aircraft, and they try to select seats on that basis. The quietest area is in front of the engines, the bumpiest nearest the tail, and the noisiest near the galleys and restrooms. The roomiest seats in the Coach class are behind bulkheads and by emergency exits. They may offer ten or more inches more leg room, even more than available in First Class. Charter flights, which add extra seats, may be over six inches less comfortable than normal airplane seating. Of course, from the tour manager's point of view, this information shouldn't be broadcast, but these seats could be allocated to taller persons or potential gripers.

Nonsmokers have to be seated in a nonsmoking area, even if this means reducing the size of the smoking area. If there aren't enough smoking seats, however, the smoker can't demand expansion, and this situation will probably require tactful handling.

Few seating arrangements are perfect. If they are window seats, perhaps they are at an odd angle for the in-flight movie. If they are aisle seats, they could be too close to the restrooms (where people congregate) or the smoking section, for nonsmokers. The tour manager should try to be considerate and equitable, and that's about all that can be done. A person cramped on an outward bound flight might be given a choice seat on the return trip. The tour manager might want to make notes of such situations, but the unhappy passenger is likely to remind the escort anyway. Tour managers should request seats at the front of the group for themselves, making for ease of checking and earlier deplaning.

During the boarding procedure, photographers may wish to exercise some of the procedures mentioned in the previous chapter. Some experts advise all those with cameras to avoid airport x-ray units, since the emissions vary and since the cumulative effect can be harmful to film. You can politely and firmly request hand inspection of film, having it readily available in cans foil-wrapping or plastic bag.

It's also a good idea to keep film out of suitcases because of radiation and the temperature of luggage compartments.

Often the airlines will let tour members board as a group. This makes it easier for the tour manager to check them aboard and to note if anyone is missing. The tour manager then boards last and, once aboard, counts again.

Intermediate Domestic Stops

If the plane stops within the United States, the tour manager must again note who gets off (if this is permitted) and then make certain these individuals get back on again. If there are absentees, the flight attendant or passenger agent must be notified. If additional tour members join the group en route, the tour manager locates them and helps them with their tickets and baggage, doing the job done by the travel agent(s) at the original departure city. These newcomers should be introduced to the other tour members at the earliest convenient time.

Many tour leaders are identified by special name tags or badges, and these command more attention from service personnel. (On a selfish note, such badges may also earn tour managers discounts in shops or preferential treatment in restaurants, but the manager must be careful about accepting such favors. Tour members could be resentful, or could suspect a fix.)

Checking Through International

Except for tour members joining the tour at the international airline desk, baggage should have been checked through from departure city to destination city and need not be hand-carried to the international carrier. However, the bags may still be weighed here, individually, or in a group. Since baggage routines vary among airlines and destinations, the tour manager should try to find out in advance what the drill will be. It's best to try to stay under the weight or measurement limits. In a sticky situation, where airline staffers demand extra money for individual overweight luggage, the offending passenger must pay this difference.

Once the tour arrives at the international airport, the tour manager must again remember to keep them together. Sometimes this means walking to the international wing; sometimes it means taking an inter-airport bus or limousine (for which the tour manager generally pays). Get everyone together, remind them where they are headed, and try to get them all on one vehicle. For large groups which must be split, assign a responsible person to see that they get off at the proper stop. No one should be allowed to stray from the group until it is checked in at international.

Once the tour members are reassembled in the international lounge, the tour manager collects the passports from tour members and brings them and the tickets to the carrier desk. Arriving at this desk early makes things much easier. The agents are not as likely to be busy and can handle the tour more efficiently, matching passports to tickets, pulling the appropriate coupons (and the tour manager should monitor this), and returning tickets and passports to the tour manager, along with boarding passes. The passports and boarding passes are given to tour members, but the ticket packets are retained by the tour manager. Again, seating should be as sensible and equitable as possible.

Tour members now wait in the general international lounge, or, if the group is small and lucky enough, in the private lounge of the airline. If there is considerable time before departure, they may be allowed to go off to visit friends, or take a cab into town. In these cases, the tour manager sets an early return time, and finds out where everyone will be. This information might include a phone number where various members can be reached. Getting such numbers enables the tour manager to place a call if the plane's departure is delayed, or if the traveler fails to show at the appointed time.

The tour manager should also get as much information as possible on the flight, including the kind of plane, meal service, movie schedule, flight time, and time of arrival. Making these details available to the passengers enhances the manager's status.

At the agreed-upon assembly time, the head count starts again. If persons are missing they should be paged, or the previously-submitted phone numbers called. Once everyone is together, they should be kept together, even if the plane doesn't leave for half an hour. Early boarding, if permitted, should be requested, and the boarding procedure is the same as on domestic flights.

Only those who have led tours can appreciate how many things can go wrong at this juncture. A tour member leaves a raincoat in the lounge, goes back to retrieve it, forgets the boarding pass, and can't get back in. Someone follows a crowd through an adjoining gate and boards the wrong aircraft. A husband goes to the restroom and his wife takes both passes aboard. So the escort must remain alert, keeping sergeant-like track of the passengers, and must stay calm. After all, this is just the beginning of the trip!

Carriers

Each method of transportation has its plus and minus features. Choices must usually be made, based on scheduling, speed, comfort, and expense.

AIRLINES

The tour escort and travel agent can minimize some flying concerns by a little passenger indoctrination beforehand. For a start, passengers may need to be sold on some of the less familiar but equally competent airlines. They know TWA and United, but they've never heard of SAA or Air-India. A few reassuring words help, and the airlines can do the rest.

Some travelers have a phobia about flying. They may never have flown before, or may have been frightened on their few routine flights, or they may have had a bad experience and quit flying. A preflight discussion of the construction and maintenance of planes, their safety features, the lengthy hours of pilot training, the preparation of flight plans, the existence of alternate landing strips, the automated back-up systems, the use of radar, and the constant links with ground control should dispel much apprehension.

When there is an emergency, such as a storm or malfunctioning equipment, the tour manager has to mask any personal fears. The stomach may be churning but the face must be calm and comforting. This minimizes the chance of hysteria or panic—or illness. Many people react wide-eyed to the slightest turbulence. While pilots frequently inform and cheer such timid travelers, the escort can also help. A smile, a wink, a shrug may communicate that all is well.

Since tour members tend to emulate their leader, it's important that the escort display interest in the routine instructions of the flight crew, including the familiar seat belt, oxygen, and flotation explanations. This way the passengers also listen. One tour manager recalls an incident when the oxygen masks dropped down, not because of any emergency, but because a switch had inadvertently been hit. "Funny thing," he said. "Even though many of us had heard the lecture dozens of times, nobody reached for the masks. We sat stunned for a few moments until the captain told us it was a mistake."

On long flights the tour manager should periodically patrol the aisles, checking to see that tour members are feeling reasonably well, and that they are comfortable (shoes off? pillow? blanket?), and that their questions get answered. This is also a good time to get to know people better.

Some travelers feel they can't be happy except on a wide-bodied plane. The big ones, like the 747 and the DC-10, can be very comfortable, but they also have their claustrophobic inside seats, and they can be a pain when everyone funnels through customs at once. Coach passengers may also resent being barred from the First Class lounge on such a plane.

Comfort can be enhanced by doing a few exercises en route, or at least getting up and walking, or stretching. Even in one's seat, it's possible to fight fatigue and stiffness by rotating the head, breathing deeply, putting pressure on the arm rests, jogging the legs up and down, rowing or apple-picking with the arms, flexing arms and shoulders, and similar exercises. Some European airlines show in-flight films of cabin exercises, or pass out literature with similar suggestions. Bantam publishes a book by Mossfeldt and Miller entitled *The SAS In-the-Chair Exercise Book.*

Another way to avoid the in-flight blahs is to eat and drink sensibly. Airline food varies. Some is prepared hurriedly, or too early, and is dry before it is served. This is further complicated by the drying action of the on-board ovens and the dehydration caused by high altitudes. Steak and fish are particularly affected by this. Some cooks also claim that foods which taste proper on land often taste bland in the air, so this calls for additional seasoning. Eating moderate amounts more often is the best idea. Special diets should be arranged before departure. Airline personnel try to discourage excessive drinking to some degree, but the escort must also be alert for tour members who tend to over-imbibe.

The best advice to give travelers who want to take photos from the plane is to sit on the shady side of the plane, in front of the wing, and shoot with their lens perpendicular to the window, and close but not touching it (to prevent vibration). Fast shutter speeds (at least 250) work better and the focus should be at infinity. If you want to establish perspective, include part of the wing in the shot. Some nations forbid photography in planes or airports, so this should be cleared with the flight crew.

During the flight, debarkation cards will be circulated. The escort may have to help some people fill these out, particularly such entries as the place where passports were issued or the address abroad. The former information should be on the individual passport; the latter may be listed as a specific place or just "touring."

When there are delays at airports, the tour manager must be a model of patience. The waiting must be made as painless as possible, and all information on departure communicated to tour members quickly and honestly. Sometimes meals may have to be arranged (normally at the airline's expense) or overnight accommodations booked. The leader should know or find out who is responsible for paying for these items, since the rules vary. If the delay is a long one, the tour manager may suggest chartering a bus to the nearest town for shopping or entertainment, may arrange for a lounge in a nearby hotel, may book in a film or a few TV sets, or can start card or other games. People should be kept together, since delays can be suddenly corrected and the flight ready to embark.

CRUISE SHIPS

The important people to know on a cruise are the chief purser and chief steward. Despite the lifestyle shown in *Love Boat,* the captain doesn't have unlimited time to spend with passengers, and he doesn't get involved in the mechanical details of tourism. The purser and the steward are better contacts.

The chief steward will work out the meal arrangements and the chief purser helps with land arrangements after debarking.

One of the first things to be done is to arrange for meals for the entire group. The second sitting is later and usually preferable. Since all dining room seating is arranged during the first few hours aboard ship, getting this handled immediately is wise. If some of the group members would rather attend another sitting, or dine alone, or join nongroup friends, let them do so.

Another important personage is the ship's baggage master who handles the luggage. One of the nice things about a cruise, from the viewpoint of escort as well as passenger, is that the baggage doesn't have to move in and out of hotels; it stays put. When the baggage is unloaded at the customs pier, the usual procedure is for each bag to be tagged alphabetically according to the passenger's name and passage class. The tour manager can ask that all bags of the tour members be tagged with the same letter sticker, so they'll be together on the pier. The letters "X" and "Z" are the most popular letters; they are also used by many tours. "W" or "J" might be better. If a bag is missing, the escort should look in the customs section under the tour member's initial.

First class passengers normally disembark first, and their luggage also leaves first. If any member of the tour group goes first class, the tour

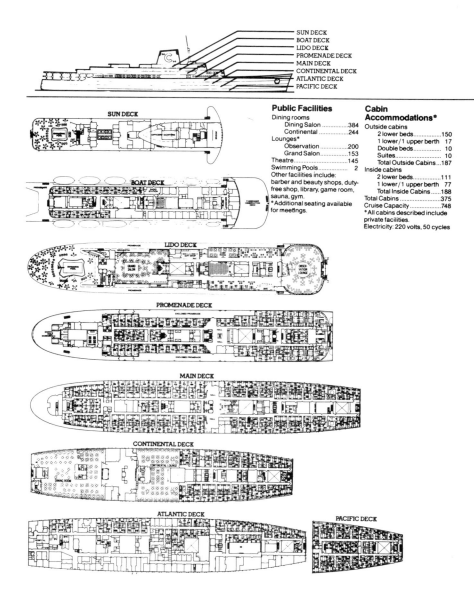

Public Facilities

Dining rooms
Dining Salon 384
Continental 244
Lounges*
Observation 200
Grand Salon................153
Theatre...............................145
Swimming Pools..................2
Other facilities include:
barber and beauty shops, duty-free shop, library, game room, sauna, gym.
*Additional seating available for meetings.

Cabin Accommodations*

Outside cabins
2 lower beds................150
1 lower/1 upper berth 17
Double beds................10
Suites...........................10
Total Outside Cabins...187
Inside cabins
2 lower beds................111
1 lower/1 upper berth 77
Total Inside Cabins......188
Total Cabins 375
Cruise Capacity 748
*All cabins described include private facilities.
Electricity: 220 volts, 50 cycles

Deck plans reproduced courtesy of Costa Cruises

manager may arrange to have all tour baggage taken off in that class or, at the very least, in the same class. Heavy baggage is usually taken from the cabins the night before docking, so tour members should be warned to be prepared to live out of their overnight bags for that final night.

As with any accommodations, there can be complaints about the cabins on cruises, even though passengers should know they get what they pay for. If there is substance to the complaint, the escort should try for an adjustment. Some tour leaders may offer to exchange cabins with the dissatisfied party, or let the passenger see that others are similarly situated, or try to make up for this lapse in some other way. A number of cruise directors suggest waiting until the second day to check on tour members' comfort. At first some travelers are surprised at the size of a cabin on board ship, but after a day these spatial concerns abate, and the tourist accepts this new way of living. This saves the tour manager at least one headache.

In addition to the chief steward, purser, and baggage master cited earlier, other individuals aboard ship can be helpful to both tour manager and passenger. Various ship's officers have duties that may interest the tourist, from navigation to communication. While they have their routine duties and may not be readily available, a polite introduction by the tour manager may provide the traveler with an opportunity to see how things run aboard.

Ship's officers may also join passengers at dinner, the bar, or at a dance. However, most ships have the regulation that they must be invited. Since there are always many more single women on cruises than single men, the ship's officers offer the only possibility of escorts. To facilitate some of this companionship, there are often "ladies' choice" dances.

In many ways, leading a cruise is much easier than conducting a land tour. Except at ports of call, passengers are contained and countable. They can't get lost, and there is no anxious waiting for them to board a bus. Since they are virtually on their own for meals and activities, there is little chaperoning or commentary required. There is also a ship's doctor to attend to illnesses, a recreation coordinator to oversee entertainment, and plenty of time for relaxing and visiting.

However, the tour manager shouldn't coast, totally ignoring the tour members. He or she should be in evidence, should be available, and should be aware of illnesses, disputes, and questions about shipboard procedures. Tour members should know how to reach their leader, and the leader must know where they are located and what sitting they attend.

Two out of three cruises are tied into jet packages, so this means scheduling must be coordinated to arrive at the dock early, but not too early. Leone von Weiss of the Hamilton Travel and Incentive Corporation recalls a time when the plane arrived late and the ship had departed. Solution? Two yachts were chartered and they caught up with the cruise ship at the first port of call. An expensive remedy, but one that certainly enhanced that company's reputation.

MOTORCOACH

When there are extra seats on a bus, the situation is more comfortable. Circulation of passengers is easier, and there is room to place bundles, or even stretch out a bit. Where conditions are more crowded, rotating seats is a good idea. This ensures that some individuals don't hog the more desirable seats; those toward the front or next to the windows. Some escorts use a numbering system and begin each touring day by announcing the seating order. Others rotate seating twice a day, moving in a counter-clockwise direction in the morning and after lunch, one row at a time. Members may exchange seats after that, but the rotation is still adhered to. Those in each row work out the problem of aisle or window locales. Some tour managers ask that passengers do this voluntarily, in order to avoid a structured sequence. Some leave the choice to a first-come-first-served rotation. However it is done, the important thing is that tour members feel they have some flexibility and aren't discriminated against.

Modern tour buses are generally comfortable and afford excellent visibility. On domestic tours, these vehicles are often equipped with restrooms and, sometimes, with wet bars or snack bars. On the typical touring bus abroad, these features would be absent, since rest and meal stops are programmed. Smoking is generally prohibited aboard the bus, although a special section in the rear may be provided, particularly if the bus is not crowded.

Tour members' luggage is loaded by the driver, since he is the expert on using space effectively. However, the tour manager should oversee this, counting the bags as they are put aboard, and making sure all make it. This also helps the escort to recognize bags, so that the absentee luggage can readily be identified.

Occasionally, bags may also be stored on the rear seats of motorcoaches. Carry-on items are generally placed in the racks above the passengers' seats or, on occasion, on the floor, or on vacant seats. These should be taken off after each day's ride. Problems arise when tour members begin to pile up purchases and, instead of mailing some home, elect to lug around bulky sweaters, giant sculptures, sacks of books, cartons of liquor, or ornate dolls. The escort can perform a service by encouraging them to mail these acquisitions as soon as feasible, even if it means paying duty.

Along with the bus driver and/or guide, the tour manager should review the itinerary as soon as possible, checking, in particular, those items which could cause problems, like places with limited facilities or too long a stretch without a stop. Establish an understanding with the driver about flexibility on stops for rests, photos, or sightseeing. Most drivers and couriers are agreeable, within reason. Some, however, may be as schedule-conscious as train conductors and need to be eased into a slower pattern.

Bus breakdowns, while rare, are a hazard. They never occur in a convenient spot, such as close to a garage. Most tour companies prepare well for such emergencies, quickly dispatching repair trucks or new buses. The tour manager, while firmly insisting on prompt rescue, must also allay the fears of tour members and minimize their opportunity for complaint. If the delay is extensive, and the situation permits, the escort might organize a short walking tour to reduce restlessness.

Bus tours have been a fixture in this country for over fifty years, starting with New York trolleys and moving onto America's dirt roads. Not only are the roads better, but most buses are heated and air-conditioned. Some are even equipped with two-way communications, sound systems, swivel chairs, carpeting, even color television.

TRAINS

In the United States, train tours today have but a shadow of their former prominence. A decade after the Second World War, they began to decline. Today, spurred by the energy crunch, trains are trying to make a comeback and compete for part of the tourist dollar.

Lawrence Youngman of Travel and Transport recently unearthed one of his company's train orders for a 1956 Farm Study Tour, from Dallas to Canada, to Seattle, and back to Dallas. The tour took two weeks, involved 15 railroad cars (including 11 sleepers) and booked nearly 200 persons. The highest priced meal en route was $3.00, and that was at a posh Canadian hotel. Dining car meals ranged from $1.50 for breakfast to $2.75 for dinner. Those days are gone forever! But train tours may pick up again.

Trains in foreign countries have survived some of America's problems. They are often the fastest and most economical way to go. And they are frequently routed to take advantage of the most spectacular scenery. Many are super-comfortable and high-speed. However, some are old and poorly equipped, lacking clean toilet facilities, air conditioning or heating, dining cars and other traditional amenities. The tour manager shouldn't approve a train on the basis of a romantic name alone and, if he or she knows the train ride will be a spartan one, the passengers should be warned. And remember, it *is* the tour manager's business to know!

Train seating is not as flexible as that on a bus, because the conductors ticket passengers in specific seats. However, people are normally free to move about, and to visit lounge and club cars. Encouraging a certain amount of movement is good.

Keeping track of tour members is relatively easy, but passengers can get tired and irritable. Even the smoothest train ride can seem long, and some are far from smooth. There can also be numerous border checks and other delays. If passengers disembark en route, they should be warned to stay close to the train. Most stops are only a few minutes. This may also pose a problem when a sizable group disembarks.

Few train stations in Europe have porters, meaning that passengers may be responsible for carrying their own luggage when they switch trains or head for taxis. This is another argument for traveling light.

The tour manager must also be in command of the meal situation. If the train has a diner, or if convenient stops are allowed, fine. If not, then the tour manager should tell the tourists to provide a little snack for themselves before departure. Sandwiches, fruit, beer, wine, or soft drinks can be purchased and carried aboard, and many Europeans travel this way to save money.

An occasional train ride on tour can be exciting, particularly for travelers who have rarely taken a train. The Canton-Hong Kong express, for example, offers wood-paneled walls, lace curtains, plants, and splendid service. It also features loudspeakers broadcasting news and military music—but these can be tuned out within each compartment.

Checking into a Foreign Country

Before disembarking from the plane or ship, the leader should remind tour members once again about the routine when entering this particular country. Go over what will happen once they land. Advise passengers to have their passports and debarkation cards ready and, when they get their luggage, to have it unlocked and ready for inspection.

The tour manager should get off ahead of the group, clear through the passport check first, and then see that others get through and head for the baggage unloading area. Here both the escort and tour members must reclaim their individual luggage. Customs may require that each person take his or her baggage through for inspection, or the group baggage could be placed on carts and taken through en masse, with spot inspection.

If any bags do not arrive, the tour escort (provided other duties don't interfere) may help the deprived passenger fill out the required forms with the airline. These forms ask for a description of the bag(s) lost, a rundown on contents, an assessment of value, and a location where the passenger may be reached, ticket number, and flight number. The passenger receives a copy of this document. If everything goes well, the missing luggage will show up at the first hotel. If it doesn't ever arrive the airlines will make a cash settlement, but this could take from six weeks to three months. If the settlement is not satisfactory, the passenger may still sue in small claims court. (A booklet, *Fly Rights,* is available from the Civil Aeronautics Board, 90 Church Street, Room 1316, New York, 10007.)

Tourists generally find (with notable exceptions) that foreign customs officers are more lenient than those in the States. Their chief concerns are alcohol, tobacco, and drugs. Most countries permit the traveler to bring in two cartons of cigarettes, or 100 cigars, or a pound of tobacco. One bottle of liquor, opened, is allowed. If questioned about any of these, the tour member should reply that he or she is carrying enough for "personal use only," and not as gifts. If a tour member is transporting restricted items either in or out of a country, that is that person's responsibility. The tour manager can't get involved in this and should in no way abet the breaking of any foreign or domestic regulation.

The tour manager should report first to the customs officials and explain that he or she has this number of tourists as part of a group. The official will then suggest either individual or group clearance. In fact, these officials have been known to wave a whole junket through the doors, saying, "Welcome to Scotland!" But don't count on it! Any talking for the group should be done by the tour manager, but only the requested information should be volunteered. Neither the tour manager nor the tour members should behave in an irritated or contentious manner with customs officials. This will only slow things up, and may result in anything from excessive baggage scrutiny to detention. Visitors are expected to cooperate.

Once customs have been cleared, or as some of the last members are clearing, the tour manager seeks out the local contact—the courier, driver, or tour operator representative. Give this person the number of tour members, the baggage count, check on the location of the bus or other transport, and then signal tour members to gather in a certain spot. Count heads and baggage once again.

The tour manager may want to allow a little time here for tour members to convert their travelers checks into local currency. This is also a good time to reconfirm flights, particularly if the stay is short. Let tour members know where the bus is located and give them a set time to conduct their affairs.

As the bags are being loaded, another count should be made. There can be many a slip twixt the terminal and the coach. Another tour may be departing at the same time and make off with a few of your bags. Or bags get picked up by airport personnel and shunted elsewhere. Perhaps this all seems overly cautious but anyone who has lost bags (and all escorts have) knows what a problem this can be. One other caution: if more than one hotel is being used for the tour group, or if more than one coach is involved, a proper separation of bags should be made so that they can be readily unloaded at the right place.

Once on board the coach, the tour manager may welcome the passengers
to this country, introduce the driver and/or courier, permitting them a few
words of greeting, and should then discuss the routine for this day and,
perhaps, for the next day. Any procedures which need review—like the
stricture about adding or subtracting luggage—should be repeated here.
Then it's off to the hotel or the ship.

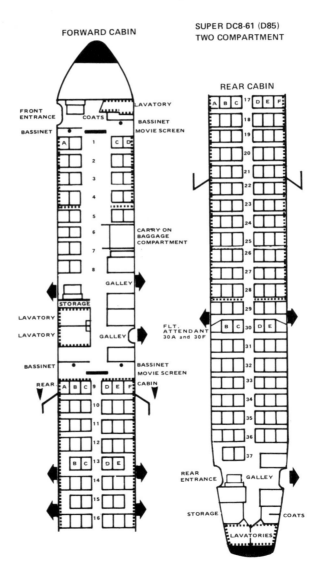

6

The Routine on Tour

Solid preparation helps launch a tour, and it also makes things run more smoothly en route. However, the human factor enters here and makes the tour proper the most sensitive part of the journey. Some of the problems encountered may be Acts of God, but most are Acts of Man (or Woman). Learning how to cope with individuals as well as situations is requisite for success as a tour manager. This means coping not only with tour members, but all the auxiliary personnel and service personnel the tour manager encounters along the way. Some of these individuals are intimately connected with the tour, while others are merely on the periphery.

The Guide

Guides are often provided by the tour operator, particularly on longer journeys, and their costs have to be built into the overall cost of the tour. These people are trained in their work, schooled in the history and culture of the country, familiar with the road system and the hotel/restaurant fraternity, and are likely to be at least semiskilled as story tellers and entertainers. While their primary functions are educational and social, they may also share managerial responsibilities, such as the details of lodging and meals.

The tour manager remains the leader, however, and must call the shots in any dispute. Obviously, he or she would be foolish to ignore the advice of someone more familiar with the country, but there are times when the manager must listen to his or her own counsel. Couriers are not infallible.

They have their own egos and their own standard procedures. They may be reluctant to venture into areas off their regular course. And they may sometimes usurp authority which belongs to the tour manager. What is needed is an understanding between these two individuals—the tour manager and the courier—and a good working relationship. This partnership can make things easier for both parties and for the tour members.

Persons who sign up for a tour often do so because of the presumed expertise of the tour manager or escort. Consequently, they expect some evidence of this on foreign shores. The tour manager can't recede into the background, relinquishing all directions, commentary, and diversion to the courier. This should be a joint endeavor, with the tour manager participating often enough to retain his or her reputation. Tactfully handled, this should cause no resentment from the courier but, even if it does occasionally interrupt the monologue, it should be pursued.

Once in a while, the courier may not read the group properly, and may have to be reminded of this. Some of the courier's stories could be offensive, or some of the commentary may be over-simplified, or the pace may be too strenuous. If the courier and tour manager have decent rapport, these matters can be handled with a minimum of friction.

Sometimes the courier handles all of the meal and hotel vouchers and does all of the tipping. The tour operator provides funds for this. If this procedure is accepted, the tour manager should check periodically and unobtrusively to see that service personnel are indeed being compensated, and that the vouchers have been properly handled. Many tour managers prefer to oversee these activities themselves, particularly if they intend to take this journey again and want to establish a personal reputation.

Normally, the courier (and driver) will be billeted in the same hotel as tour members, but crowded conditions or the whim of hotel managers may sometimes assign the courier (and driver) to nearby quarters. Since it works better to have all tour people at one location, the tour manager may make points with the courier (driver) by insisting that accommodations be found at the same place. In any event, the tour manager must know where courier and driver are staying and how they may be most easily reached. The expenses of the driver and courier are their own responsibility, and so are their housing needs. The tour manager is involved only as a courtesy, or for convenience sake.

The Driver

Many tours operate with just a driver and tour manager, with local guides helping out in key areas. The drivers are often more than drivers; they also know a lot of history, can sing, and exchange jokes. A competent and experienced escort may prefer to travel with the driver alone. This means a heavier load of commentary for the tour manager, but it can also be more fun.

The driver's main job is to get the passengers to their various destinations safely, comfortably, and on time. Baggage transfers are also the driver's responsibility, and this person may also be involved in everything from hotel and meal arrangements to narration and entertainment. Again, it depends on the capabilities of the persons involved, and their ability to work out a good relationship.

Drivers can get sulky, especially if the tour manager keeps changing the route. The driver really has no obligation to deviate from the itinerary, and the willingness to do so depends on how this matter is approached. A cooperative driver can be terrific, happily taking tour members on little side trips, or even suggesting some sightseeing beyond the limits of the itinerary. The driver should be consulted, should be asked, and should be considered.

Occasionally, the tour manager will be stuck with a poor driver, someone who may not even know the roads, let alone the local history. One tour manager recalls a New England foliage tour where the driver was working out of a cumbersome national atlas and hadn't a clue as to the detailed network of roads in Vermont and New Hampshire. However, he was an amiable fellow, so the tour manager and he just worked out the route each night and stayed on schedule. Another tour manager recalls a dour driver in Scotland, who was supposed to provide the commentary. Whatever narration occurred was sparse, often inaccurate, and certainly colorless. This chap also got lost once the border was crossed into England. This time the tour manager had a long and serious talk with the driver, and things improved. If they hadn't, the tour manager could have requested another driver.

The driver, also, works out his own housing and expenses.

The Local Guide

Major cities and some prime tourist areas frequently supply their own guides. Even when a courier may be aboard, these specialized duties are turned over to the local guide. These people are deep into the lore of the area and can get a lot said and done in a brief time. They also know local customs, the best parking spots, and the most efficient way to process large groups through heavily-populated attractions. London is an example of a city where local guides predominate.

The tour manager is fairly well locked into the itinerary of the local guide, but can make suggestions. Perhaps there is too much focus on cathedrals and shrines and not enough on other historic places. Perhaps the guide overestimates the knowledge of the tour group. Perhaps these members have some special interests, like law or agriculture, which should be satisfied. A few words with the local guide should set things right.

Most local guides know the drivers and couriers, and relate well with them. A few can be officious and demeaning. Since their stint is short, the tour manager can't do much about this rude behavior, but it can be noted later in the manager's report.

Either the tour manager or courier will introduce the local guide and let that person take over. There is little chance for any interplay because city tours move rapidly and pack in a great deal of information. It's the local guide's show. However, when tour managers perform this local function in their own cities, they must do sufficient research, run the route many times, keep detailed maps on hand, and observe local laws where a guide license is required. The tour manager may obtain such a license.

Other Personnel

Each mode of transportation has its own specialized staff, so the tour manager may have to learn to deal with conductors, museum guides, taxi drivers, or camel drovers. The basic rules, however, remain the same. Each person must understand and respect the other's expertise and responsibilities, and each must appreciate the fact that smooth, affable teamwork makes the tour pleasant for everyone.

The Routine on the Motorcoach

A time is assigned each morning for departure on a bus tour, and this information is conveyed the previous evening and possibly posted in the hotel lobby. The escort should be up well ahead of time, making certain that wake-up calls were carried out, and checking to see that tour members arrive for breakfast. In case of absentees, calls may be placed to their rooms, since some folks go right back to sleep.

If the tour is leaving the hotel and baggage is being transferred to the coach, the tour manager checks on this, even though the porters and drivers are doing the physical work. It's a good idea to walk the corridors about the time bags are supposed to be out, noting if any are not yet out. And the manager may check again as bags are being loaded, to be certain no luggage has been left in the hall. Sometimes several tours will leave at the same time, so it's helpful to have someone monitoring the tags who'll note that stray bags have joined your group, or that some of your people's luggage hasn't been collected by another driver.

After getting passengers aboard, a count should be made. You may count from the front, or walk up and down the aisles. Don't try to count while passengers are standing or getting settled. Wait until they're in their seats. And never leave until all members are accounted for.

It's important that passengers learn to respond to the departure schedule. While the tour shouldn't seem as precise as a missile countdown, it should try to adhere to the daily plan. Better to have time to squander later in the day than to lose it at the outset. Unfortunately, a few individuals are not team players. They behave as if they were on their own, wandering out to the bus ten or fifteen minutes late, sometimes sheepishly, sometimes defiantly, sometimes with incredible naivete. Often the other tour members will remind this person of the lapse, by applause, or comments, or obvious displeasure. If this doesn't result in reform, the tour manager must have a chat with the offender.

EN ROUTE

Once everyone is aboard, the coach departs, and the tour manager greets the passengers, passing on any necessary information. The driver/courier may also have a few words to say, perhaps reviewing the day's itinerary. Because some travelers like to follow the trip on their maps, a few moments could be spent outlining the precise route.

This may also be the time, particularly early in the tour, to remind people again about adding or subtracting luggage, about the value of foreign currency, or other matters that have arisen. This is also a good time to answer questions put by individuals, but which may interest the group as a whole. Luggage carried aboard must be properly stored, and removed each evening. When the coach is stopped, as for meals and sightseeing, it is usually locked and/or attended. Even so, carrying things like purses and cameras with you is a good practice. Passengers may need to be reminded of this.

Hopefully, the tour manager will soon know everyone by name, and will see that they get to know one another. Different personalities emerge, and the escort knows who can be kidded, who can come up with a rebuttal, and who needs to be drawn out. This sort of byplay helps bring a diverse group together.

The seat rotation was discussed earlier. This is the time for handling this chore—at the beginning of the day. Reminders about the prohibition of smoking, or about reserved areas for smoking, should be repeated here. (Smoking, incidentally, could turn out to be a minor problem. More than one escort has had to ask a tour member to refrain from chewing and spitting!)

Tour managers must always be conscious of safety on buses. Heavy luggage should not be stored overhead. When getting on or off, particularly at sightseeing stops, they must be extra careful. This is especially true in countries with left-hand drive. The escort should get off first and direct passengers across the road when it is clear of traffic. Although tour members are expected to stay in their seats, the escort may sometimes prowl the aisles, checking on tour members, especially those who may be having problems.

CONSULTATION AND COMMENTARY

While the tour manager may not be as familiar with the road as the driver, he or she should make every effort to project ahead. Careful scrutiny of maps, together with regular consultation with the driver, make sense. This enables the escort to help with decisions and to respond intelligently to questions.

Commentary takes experience, not only in knowing what to say but in knowing when to say it. You can't afford to ignore important landmarks, and there are also times when you'd want to make general comments, about things like native music or farming habits or domestic life. Take a look in the driver's mirror, or turn around and view the passengers. Are half of them asleep? Do you want to waken them?

Some tourists will sleep through the Brenner Pass or the ruins of the Acropolis. Touring seems to induce drowsiness, and so do heavy meals and advancing age. The commentator must decide how important it is that this information be communicated at this time. If it's the right place and the right time, go ahead, regardless of nappers. But don't waste your best shots on an inattentive group.

The courier and escort must also know how much to say. There's no need for wall-to-wall remarks. Break the presentations up, leaving ample gaps for conversation, dozing, or personal reflection. At any one time, keep comments brief. A twenty-minute monologue is disastrous. Alternate information, songs, stories, and silence. And don't force-feed passengers with your own favorite esoteric historical theories; they can't or won't take them.

One good way to break the tedium of a bus tour is by inviting audience participation. Perhaps one or two members can sing, or tell stories. Perhaps some tour member has special knowledge of an area ahead, or relatives who came from there. Let them share. This sort of activity must be controlled, since you don't want blue material, offensive ethnic jokes, boring anecdotes, or drunken reveries. Stay in charge while involving the others.

Some tours play games—typical parlor games such as Charades, Twenty Questions, or other trivia. One driver brings a racing form aboard and has passengers draw numbers on which they bet a dollar or two apiece. Then he stops enroute at some convenient tavern that's carrying the race on television and lets the tour members root home their favorites. Things like this shorten the journey.

REST STOPS

Rest and meal stops are important, and must be planned. The first rest stop usually occurs a couple of hours after departure and another will take place a few hours past lunch.

When the coach makes such a stop, sufficient time should be allowed, particularly if toilet facilities are limited. This means a halt of at least twenty to thirty minutes. If this is an area where a tip is expected for use of washroom facilities, travelers should be warned beforehand. Otherwise the tour manager may end up having to rescue a bewildered traveler from an irate washroom attendant. The location of the toilets should be pointed out, along with other places, such as coffee shops and sightseeing areas that are sited nearby. Shopping should be discouraged on these short stops, but it can't be completely cancelled. Some people will always find a shop, even on a desert.

In some small towns there are no convenient public restrooms. This means the passengers must avail themselves of the hospitality of hotels and restaurants. In this case, the tour manager should suggest they split up and not all descend on the same place. On occasion, these rest stops also include a respite at the neighborhood tavern. Some tour manuals require that the escort never take a drink during the day. Other agencies have no such policies, and the tour manager may have one drink during the pause.

Some limited flexibility may be granted on rest stops, but schedules still must be met, so excessive leeway is taboo.

PHOTO STOPS

Every tour has its photographers, casual or serious. They'll want opportunities to take pictures. This means some unplanned stops en route when photo possibilities appear. Since almost everything looks exciting and picturesque to the stranger, such pauses must be kept at a minimum. This is the price the photographer pays for the other benefits of a tour.

When a scenic spot is reached, the coach may halt and passengers be invited to take their shots. Warn them each time about crossing the road.

As soon as they've had a reasonable chance for a few pictures, signal them aboard. Nobody should take time to climb a nearby hill or wander off into the fields. Nonphotographers are usually tolerant of these stops, up to a point.

Photos taken out of a moving bus are commonly disappointing. The foreground is blurred and the composition haphazard. Suggest that photographers wait until the bus is stationary or, better still, until they can debark.

The tour manager may also want to take pictures, to bolster company files or to later share with tour members. If this is done, he or she should set an example for quick shooting and return to the bus.

One additional thought on photography. Polaroid cameras are fun to have along. While the quality of prints may not match those from better cameras, polaroids get results quickly, and offer a way to make friends with natives of a foreign country as well as with other tour members.

LUNCH STOPS

Unless the tour group is quite small and the touring area very civilized, the tour manager shouldn't figure on making a random decision about lunch. Before the day begins—preferably before the tour begins—luncheon stops should be mapped out. If possible, avoid remote places, but if the itinerary unavoidably places you in such a spot, then either pack a lunch or book lunch at some convenient facility. Arriving with forty people in a town that has only one small hotel is a serious mistake—unless the hotel has been forewarned.

Smaller groups have fewer meal problems. With a dozen or so travelers, the tour manager can arrange to stop, without specific reservations, in some community where there are several restaurants, hotels, and coffee shops. The group can then divide up and patronize a number of these. The escort should make sure, however, that these spots are clean, comfortable, reasonable, and that they serve decent food.

Breakfast is normally figured into the tour, and so are most dinners. Since both of these meals may be substantial, many tourists don't want to stuff themselves at a midday meal. That's a good reason to eliminate lunch from the tour price and let each person moderate his or her own noon repast. Besides, this makes it part of the adventure.

When lunch is part of the tour, the venue is undoubtedly set, and there is less concern with finding adequate facilities. Should a tour be running late, the tour manager or courier should call ahead to the planned lunch stop and alert them to this fact.

Allow a minimum of an hour for lunch under ideal circumstances; an hour and a half is more realistic. Passengers who finish eating early can shop or browse. Set a time for return to the coach.

Under the arrangement suggested above, travelers will be paying for their own lunches. If the meal is part of the tour, vouchers or travel service orders are used. In a case where no vouchers are available but you want to feed the group, discuss this with the restaurant or hotel management, identifying yourself and the tour, and arrange to pay later.

OTHER STOPS

Passengers must be accommodated at other times: shopping, for example, brief halts for the occasional craft shop, a chance to cash traveler checks— preferably at a time when everyone exercises this opportunity.

Often the tour members will be situated in a place where church services are available on Saturday or Sunday. It's best to attend these before the tour leaves for the day. The tour manager checks on the hours of services and the location of the church or synagogue. Then the manager tells people how to get there, if within walking distance (and after walking the route personally), or arranges for the coach to drop people off and pick them up. Every effort should be made to find compatible services for all those on tour. Whether they wish to attend or not is their business. If several churches are involved, the coach driver works out the most efficient schedule. In some instances, alternate transportation may have to be arranged by the tour member.

On occasion the schedule may allow leaving early and stopping en route for church services. If so, the tour manager had better be certain of the schedule and the travel time. One must also be careful not to inconvenience other passengers. Where it is truly difficult or impossible to work such services into the itinerary, passengers, including Catholics, are excused from the obligation.

Other stops may be permitted, like affording a traveler a chance to greet a friend or relative, or a pause at a drugstore, or a brief sojourn at a pub or coffee shop.

LENGTH OF DAILY TRIP

Tour planners should consider the endurance of passengers. The age of the group will have something to do with this. So will the amount of driving the previous day, the weather, the evening activities, the meals, and the general health and morale of the group. Don't push them.

If possible, avoid long days back-to-back. Even the most energetic, curious, and adventuresome traveler gets tired of constant movement. Schedule some shorter days, space out the free time, and arrange for multiple night stops at some hotels.

If the tour manager senses the group is getting tired, and that minor infections, like colds, are becoming common, it's time to consider slight revisions in the itinerary. A few hardy souls may be peeved, but the majority will thank you.

If you've been leaving early for several mornings in a row, schedule a later wakeup call. Green Carpet Tour managers are taught to occasionally ask for a show of hands of those who want to sleep an hour or two later—and the tour manager raises the first hand!

MISCELLANEOUS

A litter box aboard the bus helps keep things tidy and makes the driver's task easier. Good drivers police the coach every night and wash it at every convenient opportunity. This gives the tour members a feeling of being in a vehicle that is always clean and comfortable.

Peddlers and other uninvited persons should be kept off the bus. You may occasionally bring someone you know aboard, to speak a few phrases in the native language, or sing a song, or tell a story. But otherwise only tour members and tour personnel should be aboard.

If more than one coach is used, the tour manager (particularly if this person is a feature part of the trip) should divide his or her time among them. An assistant or auxiliary escort, or a courier, might alternate with the tour manager.

Hotels

Knowing the hotels on tour, and their *current* condition, is vital. The tour manager will have enough other problems without worrying about inadequate facilities. Select hotels that are sure to please just about everyone. Even then, there will be complaints.

There are hotels which the tour manager may find personally satisfactory. You may feel that the shortcomings are more than balanced by atmosphere and genial staff. But you must consider how fussy some folks can be. Going for a safer, higher-rated hotel may not be as colorful, but it spares you grief. Even those travelers who declare they wish to sample everything in the alien culture, and who react with delight when warned that a specific hotel is old and doesn't have private baths but does have character—these same people pout once they have to wait for a shower. Many tourists want to take America with them.

Hotel ratings go from Double A, to A, to B, to C—and out of sight. Some systems use star ratings. You're usually okay with the top two ratings, and probably okay with some of the next level (if you know the places personally) but facilities below these can often mean trouble. Tour operators are aware of this and rarely book Americans into anything but "A" accommodations. Even when tour managers are convinced that something less will be adequate, tour operators fight that notion. It may be neither flattering nor totally accurate to characterize Americans as spoiled and picky, but experience supports the tour operator. If the tour manager does opt for a facility that doesn't appear in the top ratings, but does offer locale and quaintness, be sure the passengers are forewarned, and blend this stay with others of superior quality.

Location must always be considered. If the hotel is situated some distance from a major city, it may be more restful and scenic, but the coach may be needed to transport tour members for entertainment or shopping. If the overnight stop is a country manor, it might well schedule its own evening program for guests, or be able to direct them to diversions in the closest village. For skiers, how far is the hotel from the lifts? For swimmers, surfers and sunbathers, how far is it from the beach? These are questions the tour manager can't ignore.

Some hotels have everything going for them. They are well-sited, clean, spacious, quiet, blessed with a congenial staff, good restaurants and bars, and with ample night life nearby. Others may lack some of these features. A little mix might work—a modern structure, then a traditional hotel, then a resort-type operation with striking scenery.

Even though the tour has been booked months before, and even though you have vouchers and letters of confirmation with you, it's still smart to call ahead to each hotel, preferably the night before, reminding them that you are coming, stating an approximate arrival time, and reviewing the length of stay and the number and type of rooms booked. You may also want to be sure they have the meals straight—the ones you'll eat at the hotel and the ones you won't.

If it turns out you'll be arriving earlier or later than discussed, another call to the hotel is in order. Early arrival means tour members may have to wait in the lobby until their rooms are ready; late arrival means at least a mixup in the meal schedule and possibly the dismal fact that rooms may have been given to others. Alert the tour members to these possibilities. The following procedure is recommended for checking into each hotel:

1. While the tour members remain on the coach (or sometimes in the hotel lobby or hospitality suite) the tour manager goes to the hotel desk and identifies himself (herself) and the name of the tour. The desk clerk produces a rooming list and the tour manager copies down the room numbers on his list (unless the hotel supplies the tour manager with a copy of their list). Make sure the singles and doubles are accurate and properly assigned, and that special requests (like rooming close to friends, or being quartered on a lower floor) are accommodated, if possible. (However, with a large group, extensive room juggling, while it pleases some individuals, may irritate those who have not made special requests.)

2. The tour manager asks where the keys are (at the desk or in the doors of the rooms); what time meals are scheduled; where the dining room, coffee shop, bar, and other amenities are located; whether there are special opening and closing times for these facilities; whether there is any mail for tour members or messages for the tour manager—and any other questions (like location of churches and times of services, or distance to town, or shopping hours) that need answers. If you need a meeting room for a tour party or special entertainment, check on this. Some international hotels require that passports be shown at check-in time. If so, the tour manager gathers these (unless the hotel insists on this being done individually), shows them, then returns them immediately to the travelers. Some hotels (like those in China) may not have keys or locked doors. And some hotels are so large that the tour manager must secure details on how the tour members will find their rooms.

3. In cases where the hotel refuses to honor reservations, or where there is a mixup in the number of singles, the tour manager should not argue with the reservations clerk. Ask to see the hotel manager, and politely, yet firmly, insist on the reservations being honored as booked. Proper documentation is the first step in making adequate adjustments. You must be armed with vouchers, letters, and other proof. With these in hand, try to get the problem solved then and there. Be persistent, since you are representing a group of clients much as a lawyer would insist on justice for an aggrieved party. If you are unsuccessful with the complaint, be certain you take down all the details, including names, dates, times, statements—everything. These may be required for later settlement of any claims. Any failure by any supplier to perform according to contract should be reported immediately to the nearest representative of the tour operator. Your driver/guide may assist with this, but you remain ul-

timately responsible. If the rooms are full, even if a culpable mistake has been made, some alternate housing is necessary. The hotel should help locate space in other comparable accommodations and should compensate the tour for any extra charges or discomfort. If alternate accommodations are in a lower class, refunds will be due the travelers. Tell them how these will be handled. All of this underscores the advisability of calling ahead.

4. Assuming all goes well, as it usually does, and the tour manager has answers for all questions, he or she returns to the group and, using the coach microphone, communicates the details to them. Ask the tour members to jot down this information, starting with times of meals (especially the next meal), location of rooms, location of keys, and times of any other functions, including any departure instructions. Then read off the room numbers, varying the order from hotel to hotel so that the same people are not always called first. Give the room numbers of the tour manager and, perhaps, the driver/guide. Any mail on hand may be distributed at this time or the passengers may be told where to get it. Sometimes hotel brochures, available at the desk, are also distributed. Then the tour members are helped off the bus, collect their keys, and go to their rooms.

5. The luggage is unloaded, marked with the proper room numbers (usually in chalk), and delivered to the tourists. This is ordinarily a job for the porters, with the driver assisting. On rare occasions, the tour manager (if able) may pitch in if there are no porters. This could happen at remote hotels early in a season, for example.

6. After tour members have checked in, the tour manager should wait in the lobby half an hour, to field any complaints or concerns. Luggage may be misdirected or missing; toilets may be flooded; lights or TV sets may not work; heat or air conditioning may be off; or other things could be wrong with the rooms. The tour manager works with the hotel staff to rectify these problems. If a tour member is dissatisfied with a room—because of size, view, or adjacent noise, for example—the tour manager will try to effect a change, and may even offer to exchange his or her own room. (Incidentally, when seeking to change a room for a guest, the useful attributes of politeness, firmness, and persistence apply. The compatibility and morale of the group, and honest advance discussions, will help blunt a lot of travelers' concerns. If they know what they are getting, it helps. The tour manager should be familiar with hotel variations and jargon. "Pensions" are characterized by modest facilities and relatively low cost; Spanish "paradors" are well-kept, more expensive, government-owned facilities; in many European countries a "bathroom" means the room has

a tub but not necessarily a toilet (you may have to specify a "water closet"); "hostal residencias" in Spain have no restaurants. Many other specialized terms should be mastered by the tour manager.

7. At the earliest convenience, probably after the bags are in the rooms and any problems have been adjusted, the tour manager should inspect the hotel, locating bars, coffee shop, hairdresser, laundry, and other amenities. This is also the time to touch base with the manager, the maitre d', and the head porter, discussing the itinerary as it affects them.

8. A convenient bulletin board in the lobby should be secured for the posting of notices about future activities. This will save the tour manager a spate of phone calls. Extra copies of the itinerary may be carried along for this purpose, or daily routines may be typed or written out. If a bulletin board is not available, an easel will do as well. Tell the travelers where these notices will be placed.

SAFETY

Veteran travelers know enough to lock their doors when in their rooms, using the dead bolt or chain in addition to the regular lock. Luggage left in the room should also be locked. Valuables, such as jewelry, extra travelers checks, and the like should be placed in the hotel safe. Tour managers often put the tour tickets in the safe, particularly during longer stays.

Emergencies like fires and civil disturbances are covered in chapter nine, but the tour manager should make an early inspection of fire exits and equipment, note any danger spots (from balky elevators to ill-placed glass windows), and alert tourists to these dangers.

This is also a time to remind people of any external perils. Some American hotels insist that tourists stay inside the lobby while waiting for a cab, and that they get right into the cab when it arrives. No loitering on the sidewalk, and no walking through the neighborhood. Some of these dangers also exist in other countries, so tourists must be wary.

CHECKOUT

Always carry a travel alarm clock. Wakeup services in hotels can go awry, and the tour manager had better be up to compensate for any failures. Some hotels have digital alarm clocks by the beds, or as part of the beds. These instruments may need explanation, so the travelers don't wake up and wonder how you turn off the buzzer or kill the flashing light. This can be done at the evening meal (after the tour manager figures it out!). After arising, go to the desk to see that the calls are being made to the tour members' rooms, or that someone is knocking on doors. Many a tour manager, rooming list in hand, has paced the corridors personally, awakening his or her tour.

At least an hour and a half should be allowed for getting ready, getting bags out for pickup, eating breakfast, and showing up at the scheduled departure time. Since some people take longer than others in getting prepared, tour members can arrange their own wakeup calls, earlier or later than the norm. However, a reminder call about an hour before departure is a good idea.

In deference to the passengers, some departure times should be later than others. Give people a chance for a few late sleeps. The schedule must be kept, of course, but make the wakeup calls as late as possible without courting scheduling disasters.

Breakfast hours on the day of departure should be arranged the previous evening, especially if this time is at variance with usual hotel procedure. This time—along with the time for bags to be put in the hall and for the coach to leave—is communicated verbally the previous day and also appears on the lobby bulletin board.

It's smart practice to have the tour members deposit their luggage outside their doors as they head for breakfast, at least forty-five minutes before departure. (If tour members are not leaving the hotel that day, but merely going on a day tour, this step is unnecessary, and an extra fifteen minutes sleep may be in order.)

At the time the wakeup calls are assigned at the desk, the tour manager should also go over the next morning's program with the head porter and restaurant manager. Shifts change, and the new people may not have been informed, so you can't check too often.

At breakfast, make a head count to see that all are up. If anyone is missing, check with this person's roommate or neighbor, or arrange to have the room called. If there is no response, check the lobby, the area outside the hotel, or knock on the door. As a final move, the porter may be called to open the door with a passkey.

The luggage is taken from the corridors by the porters and lined up in the lobby or by the coach. The tour manager should make a count of the pieces before they are loaded. After a few days, even on a sizable tour, the escort may pretty well know the bags. This is the time to catch any discrepancy. The tour manager should know where the coach is parked and may wish to schedule a brief conference each morning with the driver/courier, perhaps during or after breakfast.

After settling with the hotel, the tour manager may go to the coach. This settlement is normally in the form of a voucher. While the system varies, many tour companies make out vouchers in triplicate, keeping one for their files, sending another to the hotel in advance of arrival, and surrendering the final copy to the hotel on arrival or departure, depending on the hotel's preference.

Tour members are responsible for any extra bills they have incurred: bar bills, phone bills and the like. Once aboard the coach, the tour manager reminds tour members about any unpaid charges and asks if all keys have been turned in. Delinquent tour members should go back and settle their own accounts but the tour manager may return errant keys. The tour manager should never pay tour members' bills, nor pay for any breakage caused by tour members.

Once the luggage is tucked away, the bills paid, the staff thanked and tipped, and the passengers counted, the day's routine begins again.

Meals

Even if you can't read a French menu without embarrassment, you must be able to distinguish among the various descriptions of meals. A *continental* breakfast means rolls or toast, perhaps juice, and tea or coffee, whereas a *full* breakfast consists of eggs, meat, toast, juice, and a hot beverage. *Table d'hote* refers to a set three-course meal at a fixed, all-inclusive price, usually minus the beverage. An *American Plan* includes meals, and a *European Plan* does not. A three-course dinner normally features soup, salad, and main course, with dessert extra. Some places, of course, may not offer salads or soups. And you may have to ask for water with the meal. The tour manager must know which meals are covered by the tour and which are not, and should be familiar with the general type of menu offered.

In addition to eliminating most lunches as part of the tour price, it makes sense to consider subtracting one or more dinners during stays in large cities. Tourists like to have at least one opportunity of choosing a restaurant in London, New York, Paris, or Hong Kong.

If certain tour members require special diets, the tour manager should mention this during the advance call to the hotels, so hotel kitchens can be prepared. Most of these requests are not complicated but some may be, so ample time should be allowed.

One of the first contacts a tour manager should make at a hotel is with the maitre d'. Introduce yourself, give the number of tour members and any diet requirements, review meal times, and ask where the tour will be seated. Sometimes tour members are free to choose their own tables but often there is an established area for them, making service and control easier. Breakfast seems to be the time when groups get confused with one another, so the tour manager may want to be on hand to help direct members to the right place. Under no circumstances should the tour manager allow members to be pushed around or discriminated against because they are members of a tour. They deserve the same attention and courtesy as shown to other guests.

Meal times vary from country to country. In America breakfast is likely to be early and hearty; lunch at noon and moderate; and the evening meal from six on and heavy. In Mexico breakfast may be eaten until noon and is light; lunch begins at two or three o'clock; cocktails are served at eight and dinner at ten P.M. England's breakfasts vary, but tend toward the substantial; lunch may be the main meal, and a more modest tea replaces our dinner. Hotels catering to tourists, however, frequently adopt American standards, but British and Irish lunches are going to commence at 1:00 P.M. Things often get going much later in tropical climates.

At the first meeting with the maitre d', the tour manager may wish to extend the traditional tip, so that preferential treatment may be assured. This is particularly true when you need some special favor, like early seating, tables by the window, express service to accommodate an early curtain call, or when the group arrives late and must have special seating.

The tour escort should rotate among tables at different meals, sharing his or her companionship with everyone. If the leader pays too much attention to one or two people, even friends, others get jealous. Better to spread yourself around. Sometimes there are individuals who, because of their table manners or personalities, are fated to dine alone. Distasteful as it may be, the tour manager may have to spend a slightly greater amount of time with such persons, to temper any feeling of rejection.

The escort also shares time with cruise passengers. Ship's officers do the same, and the captain's table issues different invitations nightly. For meals ashore or afloat, tour members must be reminded to be on time. They might also be cautioned about overindulging at sea, since shipboard cuisine is usually both tempting and abundant.

Dress for meals is customarily informal, although first-class hotels and restaurants prefer to see women in dresses or dress slacks, and men in coats and ties. Even if the penalty is not ejection, the under-dressed person will feel uncomfortable. While shipboard dress is now more casual than it was, there are formal dinners, so appropriate dress should be brought along. The tour manager must set an example, and should have at least one formal outfit.

When birthdays and anniversaries occur, mealtime is an opportunity to do something special, to spend a little of the tour leader's discretionary fund. A cake is traditional and still nice, as is wine or champagne for the group. You may want to buy a card to be signed by all and, in the proper setting, a chorus of "Happy Birthday" goes over well.

Within limits, you might encourage the tour members to sample the local cuisine. There's no need to order steak and chicken everywhere. Try the rice pilaf, or escargot, or lasagna. Perhaps a soup made with lake perch and local vegetable in Hangzhou, or tapioca in various forms in Fiji. Don't insist on this, however, as you may be blamed for later nausea.

Both the tour manager and the tour members should avoid street food.

Some culinary treats offered by vendors look most appetizing, but it's better to be safe than sorry. Vine-ripened fruit, green leafy salads, and strong black coffee can be dangerous. Buffets are also risky, as are open food counters. Oranges and bananas are the best bets for fruits, and all fruits should be peeled. Other foods should be well-cooked.

Milk products could cause trouble, and the safest drinks are usually beer and major soft drinks. Water should be purified but make sure bottled water is opened in your presence. Forget about ice cubes if you are in an area where the water is suspect.

When asked about recommendations for restaurants on free nights, the tour manager should have some names at hand, but should not be over-zealous in touting specific places, since tastes differ and what is expensive to one may not be to another. Mention and describe a few, and let the tourists make up their own minds. Obviously, the tour manager should have some first-hand experience with the restaurants suggested. On occasion the tour manager may make reservations for groups, but this is not his or her responsibility. Don't lapse into the role of servant.

Watch for ripoffs in food and drink. Take note of the brands served at the hotel bars. Are tour members being charged high prices for inferior liquor? Is the food overpriced? If so, note this in your report and pass the information along to the tour operator and your own company.

Besides the normal restaurant meals, there are also events like medieval banquets or Hawaiian luau's. At least one such meal on a tour makes an excellent change of pace.

One final food note: Carry a few items like mints, gum, and cookies for distribution on the coach. Especially on long trips, where time between meals is lengthy, such goodies come in handy. When people sit for a while, they tend to get hungry, and nibbling food is appreciated.

Entertainment

Some entertainment features are expected on any tour, but there's no necessity to fill every free evening. Tour members need some quiet nights, or some personal entertainment options.

When you select entertainment in advance, try to make it varied and appropriate to the tour group. Not everyone likes ballet, but one ballet during a tour could be appreciated, particularly if the company or the stars are famous. A play—one the audience understands—provides both an intellectual and recreational dimension. Folk groups are always popular. Local entertainers may be contacted via the tour operator, the country's tourist board, the hotel, or through friends. They'll sometimes appear at the hotel, sparing the group the inconvenience of traveling.

It's not always possible to be familiar with the entertainment being offered. If in doubt, check with some authority. Otherwise you may lead your charges into a theatre where the humor is blue, the language unintelligible, the dialogue offensive, or the music loud enough to surpass the threshold of pain. Even at the Shakespeare Theatre at Stratford-on-Avon, many American visitors have difficulty with the cockney patois of the Bard's comic characters. A little advance explanation might help to avoid this.

In addition to knowing what fare awaits the traveler, the tour manager must also check the route for getting there. If the entertainment site is close, and you intend to have the group walk, then pace it off yourself in advance. Will the older members of the tour be able to go this distance? Are there steep hills? What is the neighborhood like? Are there obstructions, like railroad depressions, that require detours? What if it rains? If the coach is used, where will it park and how far will the tour members have to walk? After the performance, how do you find your coach, and how do you get your people headed in the right direction? Personal checking and planning is the key.

It's always a good idea to have the coach on standby, even when you plan to walk. A sudden storm could make the journey miserable. Good drivers anticipate problems and will show up at the theatre in bad weather even if not summoned. But the escort should not assume this; check it out!

Time is always a factor in scheduling entertainment. You must be sure you have time to work everything in. Sometimes hotels are unbending on meal schedules. Perhaps the dinner is set for 7:00 P.M. and the curtain goes up on the musical at 8:00 P.M. There is no comfortable way to enjoy both events. The tour manager must somehow arrange an earlier eating time.

Time also figures in the length of the performance and the resultant arrival back at the hotel. Older travelers can't take a succession of late nights, especially if followed by an early morning departure. If the entertainment is not structured, as at a nightclub or tavern, the tour manager may escort part of the group home early, leaving the serious revelers to find their own way back or to be picked up later. This means the tour manager must always be alert to the reactions of tour members. If they appear tired, bored, shocked, or uncomprehending, it's time to move on.

For entertainment scheduled at the hotel (a play reading, lecture, small musical group), the tour manager must arrange for an adequate room, which is often furnished free, and the needs of the entertainers must be coordinated with the facilities of the hotel. Don't leave any of this to chance. On occasion, particularly if the driver, courier, yourself, some tour member has talent, you may want to stage your own brief entertainment one evening. This pulls the group together.

Be acquainted with any free entertainment. Folk dancing on the green in front of Edinburgh Castle. A Sunday evening concert at Notre Dame in Paris. And know about entertainment with reduced prices, like those available on London threatre tickets. Or how to get into film showings at the Cannes Festival, where you must have a badge, tickets, and, sometimes, formal dress. Tour managers are expected to know these things.

Major entertainment features—plays, concerts, river cruises— should be built into the cost of the tour. Charges for other minor attractions should be handled, if possible, out of the tour manager's discretionary fund. While the escort can't exhaust these monies on added recreation, it's silly to collect fees from members each time you visit a castle or winery. In cases where a few tour members want to do something, like sailing on a lake or panning for Colorado gold, they should pay for this, even if the tour manager goes along.

In addition to varying the forms of entertainment, organized fun should also be balanced by independent fun. Let the tour members sample some of the area offerings on their own. This helps to diminish some of the feelings of constant chaperoning (for both the traveler *and* the escort), and permits the tourists to satisfy more personal entertainment tastes.

Shopping

Even though surrounded by the beauty of an evening on the Nile, some tourists are still concerned about what time the shops open in Cairo. There are travelers for whom shopping is the highlight of the trip. They want to lose themselves in the flea market, or Carnaby Street, or the native bazaars. Consequently, you must allow sufficient time for them to get this out of their systems. At the same time, however, shopping time must be controlled. Other members may resent the amount of time being allotted to this activity. There must be a blend. A few stops en route, generous lunch hours, plus some full and half days to be spent as one wishes should be ample. While it's disastrous not to allow some reasonable time for people to frequent the shops, it's just as annoying to pull up to every craft or clothing sign.

Know the days and hours that stores are open. There are national holidays and bank holidays and half holidays. Stores may close at noon and reopen later in the afternoon. They may cease business at 5:00 P.M. or remain open til 7:00 P.M. Some stores close on Monday, some on Saturday. You must check on this when making out the itinerary, and if you've calculated incorrectly you had better consider some adjustment. When people are looking forward to a day's shopping in London and they find the stores are closed, you're in deep trouble. The solution may be the re-scheduling of the next day's city tour, leaving that day free for the shoppers.

Some recommendations to tour members may be welcome, but the tour manager shouldn't be put in the position of touting specific shops. Neither should the escort follow slavishly the suggestions of the local guide or courier. These people may have their own shopkeeper friends and could get a cut for steering traffic their way. Consider such advice, of course, but be wary of promoting anything with which you're not familiar.

Warn tour members about possible ripoffs, or about shopping areas to shun at night. Hotel personnel and the local guides often provide such alerts. The tour manager can also aid the shoppers in other ways. Despite your lectures, however, some tour members will never get the local currency straight. Charts showing the various coins and bills are a terrific aid, but, even then, many tourists merely reach into their pockets, extract a handful of change, and say, "Here! Take what you want." Those who master the alien finance not only shop more wisely, they also get an ego boost.

The astute tour manager may also be able to convert sizes for female passengers. Size seven shoes become 6½ in Paris, 5½ in London, and 37½ in Rome. In ready-to-wear garments, our size ten translates into a French 42 or an Italian 44.

Even more valuable is the tour manager who can spot fakes, who knows that items using endangered species may be confiscated in customs, and who has some idea of what similar goods cost elsewhere—including in the United States. This doesn't mean, however, that the tour manager is in any way responsible for purchases or for their safe arrival home. These are the buyer's risks.

In some areas, haggling is part of economic life. Merchants expect the buyer to argue about the price and to attempt to reduce it. The tourist should have some idea about how much he or she intends to pay for an article, and whether or not this is really a bargain. Then the negotiations begin. Shepherds Tours and Travel, Inc. advises its tourists to "offer 60% of what he is asking and settle for about 25% more. . . ."

Many escorts tell tour members to buy something they like when they see it, and not wait until later in the tour hoping to find the same thing cheaper. Freeports and duty-free shops may have some bargain items, like liquor or cigarettes, but travelers often discover they can do as well or better at shops en route. In any event, it's unwise to save all one's shopping until reaching the duty-free shop at exit time. Not only may items be higher priced or unavailable, your flight could be running late and your shopping time shortened. Remember, too, that duty-free means something was imported without duty, but you may still have duty to pay when you return to the States!

Receipts should be kept for all purchases, along with the names of the stores and the personnel who waited on you. If items don't make it back to the States, you have both a contact and proof of purchase. The tour manager, even though not shopping, should note the names and addressses of major shops visited en route, since some tourists invariably need these details later.

Tourists who purchase goods in Great Britain and other European countries should be aware of the Value Added Tax (VAT) which is levied on most goods and services. Many British stores will send goods abroad free of VAT, or, for over-the-counter purchases carried in hand luggage, they will issue relief forms which have to be certified by British Customs in order to secure a tax refund. Tour managers should check details of this plan.

Finally, shoppers should be reminded periodically about the wisdom of mailing some purchases home. This spares them the problem of carting things from hotel to hotel, and from luggage packages through customs. Some travelers also use the dodge of mailing "gifts" to various neighbors and friends to escape customs duty. The tour manager should neither suggest nor condone anything illegal. However, the tour manager may advise passengers about the limit on goods ($300 in 1982) brought home before duty must be paid, and on the possibility of mailing home legitimate gifts daily, if under $25 dollars. Mark these "Unsolicited Gift." These are free of duty and tax.

Again, the local guide may be a big help, even if he or she does get a commission from certain stores. These are usually reputable places, since the guide and his or her company are also on the line. If the tour manager feels that the tour members have been cheated by any guide or any shop, this fact should be reported.

The Tour Manager at Night

Some compromise must be made between the tour manager's responsibilities toward the tour members and his or her own duties and relaxation. The escort can't ignore the group and drift off on personal business or pleasure. The manager is the group's prime contact in foreign areas and must be accessible. Even on free nights, the tour manager should be visible.

When special group entertainment is scheduled, the tour manager should always go along. Well, almost always. On occasion another emergency may require the escort's attention—some serious illness, or a threatened transportation strike. In these cases, somebody else, perhaps a mature member of the tour, should be placed in charge, and the tour manager must let them know how he or she can be reached. Some tours appoint a social director anyway from among their group. This person helps organize activities for the tour like birthday celebrations, or bridge foursomes. This doesn't relieve the tour manager of responsibilities, but it does provide a little backup while involving the tour members more in their own fun.

On nights when nothing is scheduled, the tour manager may socialize with tour members in the hotel bar, or may take small groups to different area attractions. Some travelers may wish to sample a special restaurant and invite the tour manager to accompany them. Others may wish to attend the races, or a play, or to pub hop, or merely to stroll through the village. The only caution here is that the tour manager dispense these hours of companionship somewhat equitably, alternating between the swingers who frequent the night life and the elderly who are afraid to venture far from the hotel.

Even though the tour manager is theoretically on call twenty-four hours a day, like an obstetrician, some personal time must be carved out. Regular nightly meetings with the driver and/or courier are essential. Here you plan the next couple of days, concentrating on the day ahead. Discuss any problems with the route, accommodations, entertainment, or passengers. Be open to suggestions for minor alterations. The escort also needs time to complete reports and records, to call ahead to hotels or theatres, or to phone friends or make business contacts for future trips. Since few telephone systems in the world are as efficient as in America, phoning can be a lengthy chore.

Tour managers are not immune from fatigue or illness. Yet they must look and act alive. This illusion must be bolstered by sufficient rest, so the tour manager must occasionally steal time for a nap, or relax with a book or television.

Tipping

Every tour manager seems to find tipping one of the most onerous parts of the job. You don't want to look cheap, but you don't want to overdo it. The question nags: Are you being fair or are you being taken?

The driver or the courier may actually handle the tipping, with the cost of gratuities built into the tour package price. In many ways this is a handy solution, freeing the tour manager from worrying about appropriate sums. However, it also places credit with the operator and not the agency. And the agency could be blamed for the miserly habits of the courier. If you don't do the tipping, it's a good idea to check periodically to see that this is being done. That doesn't mean spying on the courier, but merely asking occasionally, "Did he (she) take care of you?"

If you do the tipping, you may want to check with the driver or courier about local customs. In some places, offering money could be rude; in other places a satisfactory tip may be higher than you anticipated.

While things like cigarettes may be used as tips in some places, money, usually in the local currency, is the customary tip. American dollars may be used if you haven't local currency, or if the dollar is highly prized.

The agency for which you work will often supply you with its guide for tipping, spelling out amounts that should suffice. This is based on the nature and of length of the service and the number of tour members.

Allied Travel Inc., for example, makes these suggestions for tips in Great Britain:

Number of Passengers	15-29	30-45
Head waiter/main meal	£5.00	£6.00
Head concierge/per night	£2.00	£2.50
Special dinners	£5.00	£6.00
Driver - Airport Transfer	£3.00	
Harbor Transfer	£6.00	
Guide - Half Day	£3.00	
Full Day	£6.00	
Driver - Half Day	£3.00	
Full Day	£6.00	
Airport porterage - official rates:	15p per case	
Hotel porterage	15p per case	

As inflation erodes the value of the pound (or other currency), these rates will go up. Also, for exceptionally good service, you may want to boost these.

Some tipping guides go into more detail, breaking down amounts in columns for each five tour members. They also include doormen, sleeping car attendants, and personnel in nightclubs and restaurants (other than hotel). In general, the percentage of a tip for an individual service ranges between ten and fifteen per cent, with a few places (like London and Rio de Janeiro) going to twenty per cent.

Most tipping is part of the tour price and is handled by the agency or operator escort. Some tipping, however, is at the discretion of the tour member, who may seek advice from the tour manager. Since practices vary internationally, the escort should be up on local custom.

There are restroom and cloakroom tips (about 25¢), taxis (15%), hairdressers (20%), theatre ushers (25¢), waiters when meals are not included in tour (15%), and numerous cruise personnel, such as stewards who deliver meals or wine to staterooms (amounts vary among cruise lines). All of these should be tipped by the tour member, unless included in the tour.

There are differences among countries. Restaurants tips, for example, vary from zero in China to 25% (usually added to the bill) in Buenos Aires.

Tipping of any kind in China is considered rude, and in Japan, many service people, like doormen and chambermaids and taxi drivers, do not expect tips. Tipping in Russia and India is very minor, with 5% in Moscow acceptable. Service personnel in Rome and Paris expect visitors to be generous. So know where you are.

It is customary to tip both the tour guide and the driver, even though both are paid by their company. Some agencies suggest that this be left to the tour members, while others suggest a tip from the tour manager's expense fund, regardless of what passengers do.

Whatever the passengers elect to do should be at their discretion. The tour manager should neither encourage nor promote such a collection. Many travel agencies recommend individual tipping by tour members rather than making up a pot of money. The latter process, however, is common. In that case, the passengers elect a spokesperson who presents the purse to the courier and/or driver.

The typical formula for the tour guide (or courier) might be at least a dollar a day per person, or a minimum of $15 per person on a two-week trip with the same person. A customary tip for the driver would be half that. Where the driver also assumes duties of the courier, go with the larger amount. Remember, however, that the tour manager stays out of this, and what they wish to give (if anything) is up to the tour members.

Sometimes the tour members may also wish to make a gift to the tour manager. This should be discouraged. Any money should be refused, unless such refusal would be awkward or cause hard feelings. A small gift might be preferable, but the tour manager should tactfully let the passengers know that such rewards are neither expected nor appropriate.

A few final points:

- Always check to see if the service charge is already included on the bill.
- If visiting several countries, you might make up tip packets in the local currency for this specific purpose.
- Don't be afraid to exceed the recommended amounts, particularly when someone does you a special favor, like advancing the time of a meal.
- If confronted with surly and grasping personnel at a hotel or other stop, report this in your tour-end summary.

The Cruise

As with the hotel, the tour manager should try to be as familiar as possible with the ship chosen for a cruise. At the very least, the manager should review deck plans and photos and should speak with professionals who have used this line. Much better, of course, is a personal visit to the ship, either on a familiarization trip, a previous voyage, or just prior to embarkation. This tour will familiarize the escort with the cabin arrangements and the various public areas. Sometimes the tour manager may be supplied the stateroom arrangements in advance, enabling him or her to enter these on the personal manifest and on the deck plan.

Obviously, the tour manager must be acquainted with the fundamental terms of nautical jargon. Even landlubbers know you're on a ship, not a boat, and that left and right are port and starboard. The back of the ship is aft (or the stern) while the front is forward (or the bow). There are decks, not floors, and when you descend you go below, not downstairs. The tour manager must know the names of the decks, from Sun to D, or whatever designation the ship makes. There's no need to overdo this, greeting tour members with "avast" or "ahoy," but cruising is one of those specialties, like sampling wine, which calls for its own vocabulary. Mistakes stand out.

Baggage is less of a problem than on air/bus tours. The passenger keeps his or her own baggage identification. For most tours a couple of suitacses suffice. These are brought to the dock by the tourists and carried aboard by porters. Other luggage, like steamer trunks, which may be shipped but not used en route, is tagged and handled separately.

Boarding a ship is not as fast as boarding a plane. Three or four hours may be required, and the tour manager should be on hand during this entire time. While the crew may issue stateroom assignments, the tour manager (who could be at a desk furnished by the cruise line) assists with problems, greets tour members, and helps them locate their cabins.

A tour member who wishes to move up to a better class of stateroom must pay extra for this privilege. Once aboard, changing may be difficult, since cruises are often booked solidly. If the passenger does switch, be sure you make this change on your roster.

The main meal aboard the ship is dinner. Many passengers dress formally for this occasion, and this is mandatory on some cruises. Details about dress (and other things, from passport requirements to embarkation procedures) are found in brochures supplied by each cruise line. If such brochures are not supplied, check with the travel agency and pass this information on to tour members in advance of their leaving their own hometowns.

Dress for most other meals is informal, but special events like the Captain's Dinner or the Captain's Cocktail Party call for more formal apparel. The tour manager should certainly set the tone for the group. Breakfast and lunch are likely to be open seating, and you may even order a buffet lunch by the pool, without changing from your swimsuit.

Meals are good occasions to check on tour members, especially on large ships, just to see how they are faring. If unable to spot a tour member at a couple of consecutive meals, the tour manager should check with others, or knock on the stateroom door.

Many ships book big name entertainers for the evening shows. They also feature movies, dances, organized games, and theme parties. In addition, sports opportunities abound: pool, shuffleboard, swimming, ping pong, deck tennis, skeet, lifting weights. The tour manager may help get tour members involved, and, health and talent permitting, join in the activities.

During entertainment in the lounge or salon, the escort will want to be present, and should circulate among tour members, buying an occasional drink for different individuals. Holding a party each week for the tour group is another nice idea and not too expensive. The advice on spending time with varied groups also applies to shore excursions. The tour manager is under no real obligation to accompany members on optional shore visits, but such a presence is helpful.

Steamboat and river cruises share some similarities with ocean trips, but the entertainment features are fewer and the shore excursions less of a

Photograph courtesy of Costa Cruises

problem. The atmosphere is even more informal at meals, and because the ships are considerably smaller keeping track of people is much simpler.

Most tipping aboard ship is a passenger concern. It's customary to tip at the end of the voyage, as at the last meal for dining room personnel and the day before docking for stateroom attendants and other personnel. Bar tipping is done when drinks are bought.

Other Forms Of Tours

Veteran escorts will tell you the toughest kind of tour to lead is a long cross-country bus ride. Distances are great and there are often long stretches without much scenery worth commenting on. The long bus tour is a test for the tour manager, who must have exceptional patience, energy, and personality. On some tours the escort may want to nap early and then stay awake while others are sleeping, just to keep the driver company. Sufficient rest stops are also a must.

There are many forms of tours: raft trips, two or three day trail rides, and even camel caravans. The tour manager must adapt, remembering the need to provide all the necessities for tour members, along with a good time. Heads must still be counted, illnesses attended, disputes settled, and commitments met.

Miscellaneous

OPTIONAL TOURS

When tour members do have free time, they may ask the tour leader for suggestions. So the tour leader should have some ideas, or even brochures. At least three options should be available. These should be side trips or events or special places the tour manager knows about personally or from very reliable sources. Don't recommend anything about which you're uncertain. Always know which people have gone on special tours and how you can reach them. Also, check them in on return.

LOCAL TOURS

When taking a local tour, particularly in major cities, the tour manager should be conscious of the possibility of members getting lost. Some castles, museums, and cathedrals are jammed and it's difficult to hold a group together. A colorful hat (preferably on a tall member of the group), a pennant on an umbrella, or some other rallying symbol should be employed. If the local guide leads, the tour manager should bring up the rear, keeping folks together. If the head of the group moves too fast for the slower tourists, shout for the leaders to slow down.

TEMPORARY DEPARTURES FROM THE TOUR

On occasion tour members may wish to leave the tour at some point and join it later. Perhaps they wish to visit relatives or friends, play golf, fish, or conduct some business. They may even wish to see something not on the tour. Unless this alteration appears dangerous or inconvenient, the tour manager may allow it. However, the departing member is responsible for his or her own welfare, expenses, and return. The tour manager will, as before, want to know where the person is going and who to contact in case of emergency.

Tour leaders who are very familiar with a country and who have many friends there are often able to fullfill a special request of a passenger to experience some particular thing. Perhaps a physician wants to meet another physician, or an attorney wants to visit a law court, or a farmer wants to discuss irrigation. Setting such meetings up is a real plus for the member.

EUROPEAN RAIL TICKETS

European rail tickets can sometimes get complicated. Separate journeys on the same rail line may appear on a single ticket, so you must hang on to the tickets. On tours, the tour manager may carry a single ticket with the names of tour members, plus small stubs or counterfoils to be surrendered to conductors. While customs differ, the best single piece of advice is hang on to the tickets!

BORDER CROSSINGS

Let the local guide or courier handle things when crossing from one country to another. Passengers should be advised to remain quiet and to cooperate with the authorities. This is no time for flippancy or belligerence. Misconduct may lead to a thorough and lengthy search of baggage, or even to detention. Sometimes the check is perfunctory and the guard may wave the coach or train right through. At other times there may be a passport or luggage check of some intensity.

LOCAL CUSTOMS

In the same vein, passengers should be instructed to respect local customs. If the Vatican has certain restrictions on dress, they should be obeyed. If a site is considered too holy to be photographed, refrain from taking pictures. If women are not allowed in certain bars, don't make an issue of it. Go with the flow.

In China, hotel doors are typically left unlocked. Shorts are not worn. Sightseeing is strenuous. Tardiness is considered very rude. Evangelical literature will be confiscated. Talking with your hands in your pockets is disrespectful in Germany. And you should never squeeze a fraulein's hand too firmly in greeting. Never take chrysanthemums as a gift to a Belgian home. Those flowers are reserved for funerals. And these tips merely scratch the surface.

TAXES

In addition to knowing foreign currency, the tour manager should be aware of taxing systems in various countries. If there is a Value Added Tax, for example, explain this to the tourists. If there are departure taxes at airports, (which are not included in the tour) budget for these. If you stay at some American hotels with a lodging tax, note this.

YOUTH GROUPS

Most tours cater to adults, often older adults. But there are youth tours which, from the tour manager's viewpoint, have plus and minus aspects. You have fewer problems with illness, and it is often more fun to be with a lively, congenial group. But accommodations will be more spartan, food less elegant, and entertainment more youth-oriented. The biggest problem is that young people are less likely to appreciate being led. They are more apt to stray. There are more problems with discipline, romance, occasionally with drugs—but usually less problems with drinking or with complaints.

Youth tour leadership requires special talents. While being able to get along with young people, the escort must also command their respect. He or she must know when to be flexible and when to be firm.

DISPUTES AND REFUNDS

The policy on refunds is spelled out in the brochure and itinerary passengers receive. In general, there are no refunds once the tour starts, except in most unusual circumstances. Bills have to be paid as contracted, even if a tour member must leave for illness or is sent home because of disciplinary reasons.

Individuals who want to skip a meal or a play or some other feature of a tour are not entitled to refunds. The food and fun are available to them; if they choose to forego them, that's their choice.

The tour manager should never engage in a dispute with a tour member over what has been paid for. If a tour member insists he's paid for some optional item on the tour, but you have no record of this, permit the individual to enjoy that item, telling him politely you'll check it all out later. Put this in your report and settle it when you return to the States. Public arguments about things like this make the situation uncomfortable for all concerned.

7

A Tour Is a Group of Individuals

No matter how hard you work at promoting collegiality among tour members, you are still going to wind up with a fairly diverse set of personalities and temperaments. This is not a family; it's not a team; it's a group of distinct individuals. Each tour is different. Sometimes there is a spirit of camaraderie that pervades all activities. The people like each other and function together. This is the ideal. A more likely situation is that you'll have a high percentage of nice folks and a few mavericks. Hopefully, the influence of the latter can be kept to a minimum.

The size and nature of tours has some impact on personalities. The smaller the group, the more the chance of cooperation and congeniality. Larger groups offer more opportunities for disagreeable characters. Tours into problem areas, a succession of rainy days, a multiplication of housing problems, contagious illness—these can all turn a pleasant crowd sour.

On some tours there are individuals who should never have booked this type of excursion. The pace is too fast, or the accommodations below their expectations, or the entertainment dull. All you can do in cases like this is to try to make them marginally happy, and hope they'll shape up. In fairness to tourists, it should be repeated that most of them are delightful traveling companions. You'll have the 81-year-old woman who is the life of the party. Or the handicapped person who inspires others and blunts complaints. Or the couple who tell you every night what a lovely day they've had. Most travelers are grateful to you and the driver/courier for all you add to their traveling pleasure.

But you do encounter problem people, and because you are destined to live closely with one another for a few weeks, these characters stand out. The idiosyncrasies are legion, but here, in alphabetical form, are some of the difficult tourist types:

Tourist Types—From A to Z and Beyond

The Abusive Individual People who are insecure themselves, or who are consumed with personal trials, often take out their anger on fellow passengers. They also hassle hotel and restaurant personnel, and openly criticize the tour manager's performance. Their response to friendly overtures is hostile. They are unhappy and they want to make others unhappy. The tour manager cannot tolerate this behavior. A talk with the person(s) is the first step. They must understand they will not be allowed to ruin this trip for others. If this lecture fails to bring about reform, they must be dismissed from the tour, regardless of the scene this may cause.

The Bore There are boring people in all walks of life—at work, at parties, in the neighborhood. However, on a tour, these annoying people can hardly be avoided. You are closeted with each other for long periods of time. Fellow passengers don't want to hear for the umpteenth time how he once met Johnny Carson or how she decorated the family room.

Some bores can be aggressive, and have to be dealt with bluntly. Often they are basically good people who just get carried away. Try to kid them out of this nonstop chatter. Or direct conversation a bit more, not allowing the bore to monopolize things. As with other personality problems, the remaining tour members may actually solve this dilemma for you. By avoiding the bore, they sometimes teach him or her a lesson.

The Chronic Complainer Nothing suits some folks. Everything is probably better elsewhere. The hotels are shabby, the meals nearly inedible (although they eat everything but the napkins), the motorcoach too hot or too cold, the other passengers aloof, and the entertainment either inane or disgusting. They either never read the brochure or they read every word. If you alter the itinerary at all, even to add a superior attraction, they will protest. "That's the one thing I came to Austria to see!" This statement is made even if you have eliminated one of a dozen craft shops, or an early morning glimpse of a granary. If the complaints are personally annoying but not destructive of morale, you may tolerate them. If they undermine your leadership, or threaten your sanity, dismissal from the tour may be the only alternative. (First, however, you'd better check the guidelines of your tour operator to see if there are any problems with this remedy.)

The Drunk You can often spot potential drinking problems at the pretour party. People get high, loud, and cantankerous. A noisy drunk is more of a problem than a quiet drunk, and both are easier to deal with than the drunken couple feuding with each other.

"I had this couple," says one tour manager," and they were smashed every night, and some of the days. Worse than that, they fought all the time, using vile language to each other. And they even got pretty physical, shoving each other around. I called them in and told them I was sending them home. They begged to stay on, and promised to reform. For a few days they were okay. Then, when we were flying from Tokyo to Hawaii, they got into a fight, and he threw food at her, and jumped up in the aisle shouting. The airline stewards dragged him into another seat and held him there. Then we dumped them both off the tour in Hawaii."

Another tour manager reports doing the same thing in Los Angeles, on a trip from Hawaii to Chicago.

Still another tour manager recalls a man who was drunk from morning until night, and who was loudly critical of the tour and the way she was handling it. She spoke with him and he did reform. To be sure, however, she went into the bars of every hotel they occupied and told them to serve this man nothing stronger than orange juice.

"I had one man get very drunk on the plane," recalls an escort from a West Coast agency. "He got sick, vomited, and couldn't even sit up straight. I told the airlines people, 'You got him this way; now you figure out how to get him off!' We wheeled him through customs."

There are also groups of drunks, friends that take the trip together and who start off with Bloody Marys in the A.M. and conclude with scotch and water in the evening. If they can keep themselves under control, no problem. If not, the old heart-to-heart talk must be unveiled. Heavy drinkers can't be allowed to terrorize or embarrass others, to insult service personnel, or to disrupt in any way the smooth course of the tour.

The Elderly Person Older people are usually the best travelers. They probably have a lot of spirit, or they wouldn't be along. Many of them know their own limitations and settle for remaining behind during any strenuous activity, like climbing eighty-five stairs to the turret of a castle.

Some, however, may need constant watching. They stray into traffic, get lost during shopping sprees, fail to remember instructions, or become ill. Since packaged tours tend to attract older citizens, the tour manager must know how to deal with them as a public. This means everything from speaking up a little louder to exhibiting patience with their infirmities. These qualms aside, most tour managers seem to enjoy the senior crowd, and they certainly appear to be more grateful for services rendered.

The First-Time Traveler If the neophyte tourist is willing to listen and learn, there need be no difficulty. The problem arises when the first-time traveler, ignorant of the routine, fails to take advice or refuses to learn by experience, and makes the same mistakes over and over again.

The first-time traveler will harbor more fears. Fear of airplanes, fear of ships, fear of not making friends, fear of getting stranded, fear of getting sick, fear of losing money or travelers checks. This person needs added reassurance. Be tolerant; be willing to repeat.

The Gossip Male or female, this person likes to spread rumors about others on the trip. These tales may encompass past behavior of fellow passengers, current romances or imagined romances, drinking habits, and other matters. The tour manager should make it perfectly clear that such tale-bearing is not appreciated and, if this gets out of hand, should have a frank talk with the offender and insist that such conversation be discontinued.

The Hypochondriac Travelers do get sick, of course, and some may have serious health problems and should have been discouraged from taking the trip in the first place. Some passengers, however, are hypochondriacs; they imagine every ache and pain as fatal. A stomach ache is translated into an ulcer attack. A sprain becomes a broken bone. One tour just arrived in Paris from New York and checking in had barely been completed when one man came to the tour manager and said:

"I'll have to go home."

"Go home? You just got here!"

"I know, but I have to go home anyway."

"What's the problem?"

"Hemorrhoids. They're acting up. And I can't spend three weeks sitting on a bus."

He finally agreed to see a French physician and continued on tour. Every few days, however, brought inquiries about the possibility of going home. Once the tour manager had even made reservations, from Brussels. The victim endured, finished the journey, and told friends afterwards that it was the finest trip he'd made in his life. His wife, incidentally, was cool about the whole thing, ignoring his complaints. She'd been through this too often.

Another incident occurred in Edinburgh when a passenger adamantly declined to enter a Protestant church, remarking that no one in her family had been in such a place for generations. Coaxed into entering anyway, she slipped on the wet flagstones and sprained her ankle.

"I knew it, I knew it," she cried out in guilt.

The ankle healed quickly, but her limb, swathed in Ace bandages, gave her an excuse to monopolize the front seat, with her leg propped up.

When a person complains about being ill, always insist they see a physician. Don't put up with complaints if the person won't take any steps to relieve the symptoms. The difficulty is distinguishing between those who do require medical assistance, and those who are using this device to get attention.

The Introvert Timid, insecure travelers don't want to leave the escort's side. They are nearly umbilical. Encourage them to break loose. Ask others to include them in their activities. There are usually a couple of motherly or fatherly types aboard who welcome this opportunity. A little kidding sometimes helps, and makes the introvert feel noticed and wanted. Find some way to pair this person up with others.

The Junior Exec. It's not fair to categorize all junior executives as problem cases—but some are. A little power goes a long way with certain individuals. In the office they rank low in the pecking order, but on tour, where nobody knows their true position, they tend to exaggerate their importance. They want to impress and dominate. They expect a little pampering. Give them a little—very little. Don't let them put you down, and don't let them make quieter members uncomfortable.

The Knocker This person differs from the complainer in that the knocker picks apart the tour and its leadership, not by way of complaint, but to massage his or her own ego. They've always seen something more spectacular, stayed at finer hotels, eaten fancier meals, and toured under better guides. Ignore them. Personalities like this eventually grate on everyone, and their persistent cynicism makes no converts.

The Lover This is a particular problem today, when the rules of sexual conduct are pretty relaxed. Things you might have scolded individuals about in the past are now commonplace. A man and a woman book separate rooms, but spend the nights together. What can you do about this? Probably nothing.

Some women leave notes and keys for the guides or drivers. Some guides make a play for the single women. You can't do much about the tour members, but you sure can have a talk with the courier or driver. Tell him (or her) to cool it. Some drivers, in an attempt to charm, carry things too far, and some lonely person mistakes this attention for romance. Break up this affair.

When the situation involves two passengers, that's another matter. You may intervene, but veteran tour managers say you should ignore this, as long as the couple is discreet. If one of the parties is a personal friend, you may want to issue a friendly warning, but things like this get pretty sticky.

It goes without saying that the tour manager must be above reproach in such relationships. No fooling around.

The Moody One You don't expect everyone to radiate sunshine, but the perpetual grouch is both unnecessary and unwelcome. To him or her it's not a good morning, and the weather is not pleasant, and the scenery is dull. This person is still angry about some past event, perhaps something that occurred years ago. Be cheerful with this person, ignoring the choler. This approach may be partially contagious and, if not, it will still make you feel better.

The Nosey One Some tour members check on the times others get to bed, arise, on how much they drink, on who they are with. They even keep track of the vegetables they like and dislike on the menu. Never show any interest in such prying. And, if others are disturbed by this behavior, suggest that the snoop butt out.

The Organizer This individual wants to take over the tour. He or she feels you should be doing something different, covering an alternate route, enjoying a better play, or leaving the hotel at a different time. These people are annoying to other members, and they'll watch to see how you handle this challenge to your authority. At first, you may pleasantly assure this person that you have things under control. If this doesn't work, then it's back to the private talk.

The Pure American For this tour member, everything is superior in the United States. We have better facilities, more spectacular vistas, and, certainly, better food. This individual wants to take America along. Foreign dirt is always dirtier, and foreign food strange and inedible. They'll ask, "Haven't you got any good American food, like hamburgers?" when you're dining at a classy restaurant. They keep asking for 7-Up and ice cream, or some off-brand of Kentucky bourbon. Once again, patience is called for. Joke with them; make them realize how silly they sound; introduce them to new experiences, even when they resist.

The Questioner This tourist never listens. The tour manager or guide announces that the field to your left is Runnymede, where King John was forced by his barons to sign the Magna Charta in 1215. A few beats later a tour member asks what that place is. The guide patiently explains that it is Runnymede. "What happened there?" "The Magna Charta was signed." "By whom?" The guide or tour manager will eventually just state that this was already covered by the commentator, and that the questioner should pay closer attention. Convey this rebuke in a gentle way, not as a scolding. But don't keep repeating, as this exasperates other travelers.

The Rebel Instead of conforming to the conduct of others, the rebel marches to a different drummer. He doesn't want to go along on the Pearl Harbor cruise; he'd rather take a plane to Maui. She doesn't want to go to the Sydney opera, and tries to recruit some friends for pub crawling. To some degree, this independence can be tolerated, but not when every day brings some new adjustment, and not when these contrary actions are beginning to influence others. Make it clear, too, that any divergence from the itinerary is at the rebel's own expense and risk. And the tour won't be inconvenienced in any way. You want to avoid a messy confrontation, but you must remain in charge.

The Shopper Although a certain amount of shopping is absolutely necesssry, it can be overdone. Some tourists want to visit every roadside stand, and virtually pout when you must pass. If you make a rest stop, they may disappear into nearby shops and keep the tour waiting fifteen or twenty minutes. Warn them about this and, if they don't return on time or respond to the honking bus horn, get the coach rolling.

"On a recent Sun Country Tour," reports a tour manager," two ladies insisted on spending extra hours in Scottsdale in order to do some shopping. The escort explained (politely but firmly) the motorcoach must proceed as scheduled in order to include all the sightseeing the brochure outlined on the 12th day. The ladies were most unhappy and would not converse with anyone. When they arrived in Flagstaff they were so impressed with their Little America accommodations they made a point to apologize in front of the group."

Would that all tales had such a happy ending!

The Troublemaker There's a mean streak in some folks that prompts them to get their kicks out of making others unhappy. If there is nothing negative happening, they'll make it happen. They like to argue, or pick fights, or pit tour members against each other. They are rude to fellow passengers and to service personnel. They like to see things in an uproar. Cut them off at the pass. At the first sign of this mischief, call them aside and read them the riot act.

The Uncouth Individual With a diverse crowd, you should be on your best social behavior. Individuals who sprinkle their speech with profanity or vulgarity, or who tell a succession of dirty jokes, are a nuisance. A few folks are just earthy, and their conversation, while a bit raw, may be colorful. Others are just gross.

Some have stomach-churning eating habits, slurping soup, chewing loudly, belching. Some take their teeth out and set them on the table, or they discuss the condition of their bowels during dessert. One woman on tour carried around the kidney of her deceased husband, and would show it to others at the most unlikely moment. Some people, too, are personally unclean, or have bad breath, or possess other traits which are the target of late night TV ads.

All of these are ticklish situations. If the guilty party has a friend through whom you can communicate a message, use this route. You can also hope that treatment from other passengers will wise up this clod. If nothing like this good fortune occurs, the old dismissal may be invoked. But be careful. This could be the basis of a lawsuit.

The Veteran He's seen this movie before, and he wants to reveal the plot. While the guide is trying to comment on the landscape, the veteran anticipates and tries to top the guide's performance. Even when the terrain is new, the veteran interrupts with not-so-quiet asides regarding more unusual sights he or she has seen. Treat this person as a harmless but unruly student. Ask if this person has something to say that all might benefit from, or simply request silence during the commentary, so that others may hear.

The Wanderer A common difficulty on tour are persons who are either late or lost. They may have a hard time getting up in the morning, or they may resist direction, or they just may not care what others think or feel. Whatever the motive, the result is the same. They delay the entire tour. A little pressure from fellow passengers, some gentle reminders from the tour manager— these should correct tardiness.

Lost tour members form another problem area. You're ready to leave and the women are in the bathroom and the men in the bar. They're not really lost, but you still have to locate them. Sometimes they are genuinely astray. They take a walk, turn the wrong way, and can't find the route back to the hotel. Warn them about this. Have them remember the name of the hotel and some landmark. Even then, it may not work.

Three women went for a walk in Kendal, England, one night. They were given instructions about the hotel name and a landmark. In less than an hour, they were lost—and they all forgot the name of the hotel. Fortunately for them, all the natives here speak English. They stopped one and asked for help. He asked if they could remember a landmark. One recalled a bell tower.

"My dear lady," the Englishman said, "there are twelve bell towers in this city. Can you remember any sign? A street sign, perhaps?"

They thought a while and one lady brightened.

"Yes," she said. "Toilet Street."

She recalled the sign for the public lavatory in Kendal. Surprisingly, the Englishman put the bell tower and sign together, and showed them the way to their hotel.

Try to impress on tour members that, like Hansel and Gretel, they should always try to mark the trail back. A match box, hotel card or other identification could also be carried by sightseeing travelers and checked if they get lost.

The Expert A mine of misinformation, that's the so-called "expert." This person ladles out erroneous data on currency exchange, false historical information, wrong times for departure, fabricated reasons for any delays. He or she pretends to know everything. Not only are such persons misleading, they also add to the questions the tour manager must answer. Challenge them, and silence them.

Young Children Some kids are a joy; others are no fun at all. On most adult tours, youngsters will be bored. They keep wanting to know when you are going to eat, or stop, or get back to the hotel. They have to go to the bathroom fifteen minutes after a rest stop.

"I had a kid who pulled this on me several times," says one tour manager. "I'd tell her to be sure to go to the bathroom before we left, but she wouldn't. One day I just had the bus stop in the middle of nowhere, with a few trees and bushes, and said, 'There you are. Go there. We can't stop in any towns for a couple of hours.' I had no more problems after that."

Kids also have fussy eating habits, may find the entertainment above them, and can get a lot of colds and stomach aches. But they can also liven things up. Children who can smile through some tough period, like a bus breakdown or a long airline delay, make the other passengers feel sheepish about their complaints.

The Zealot Those who spend all their waking hours promoting a cause may make excellent crusaders, but they are a menace on a trip. The tour manager should personally avoid any discussion of religion or politics, and should intervene in any heated discussion on these or other volatile topics. People live too closely together on tour to be preached at.

Those are only twenty-six problem cases. There are many more. The women (or men) who wear noxious perfume, for example. One tour leader wrote:

"At the start of a 36-day tour of Canada and the United States, with 40 tour members, a lady came to me to complain that, because of allergies, she would not be able to tolerate the fragrance another woman passenger was wearing. She thought the woman had bathed in her toilet water that morning. I told her I'd take care of it and, after much thought, I took the mike and proceeded to advise *everyone*: 'Because this tour is a first for most of you, to make it as comfortable as possible, may I ask that you try to keep your fragrances to a bare minimum. Aftershave lotion, hair sprays, and colognes can be annoying in the close confines of a bus or plane.' It worked so well, even I was afraid to use my hand lotion for fear of offending."

There are thieves who rifle through hand luggage, or lift gifts; customs evaders who put the whole group under suspicion; and camera nuts who take embarrassing photos of fellow tourists.

There are also squabbling roommates. They may have been friends for years, or they may have paired up at the get-acquainted party. Now they can't stand each other, and they want you to settle things. If possible, you might pair them up with other singles. If this doesn't work, suggest single rooms (if available), for which they must pay the extra charge. If no change is possible, just tell them the arguments must cease, and they must try to get along like mature adults, They may avoid each other as much as they can, and this cuts down on public displays, at least.

If a roommate snores and the other person can't sleep, you really should arrange for another room, if not at that hotel, then somewhere nearby.

Handicapped persons represent a special challenge and there are tours that cater to them, selecting hotels that have special ramps and doors and other items. Rambling Tours, for example, welcomes those in wheelchairs or with canes. They even have an "electric elevator" to simplify getting on and off the coach. And they assure their tour members that they know how to handle emergencies, and how to summon prompt medical assistance.

Group Psychology

There are courses, seminars, and books on mass psychology. These help. So do things like experience and common sense. While you can't know too much, regardless of the source, an astute tour manager will pick up a great deal of knowledge by just observing passengers. Put yourself in the other person's place. What would you want at this point in the tour? What would you be thinking about? That's a start.

Remember that your job is to exercise control over the group while satisfying their expectations and insuring their enjoyment. You have a captive audience. And you have an advantage—they have certain fears they feel you will assuage. They don't want to strike out on their own. You know the routine, and they trust you. They may test you to see how you react to pressure, but they don't normally want your responsibility.

You should be pleasant without being saccharine, and politely firm without being dictatorial. This requires ingenuity and patience, but nobody said the job of tour manager was easy!

Here are some reminders:

- *Establish relationships early* Even at the get-acquainted party, let members know you are in charge. Size them up, too, speculating on potential problems. This initial impression isn't infallible, but with a little practice you can get good at it.

- *Play no favorites* Spread yourself around. Be friendly, but don't mislead anyone, and don't make others jealous.

- *Be respectful, but not servile* You are a gentlemen or a lady, not a servant. You don't run out for cigarettes on demand, or perform other menial tasks for travelers. Be helpful, but not docile.

- *Be sensitive to moods* Pick up the signals, the comments, the body language. Know when tour members are tired, bored, anxious, afraid, hungry, thirsty, angry, suspicious, or whatever. Pace yourself and the tour to these prevailing moods.

- *Lead without compulsion* Never seem to be forcing things. Make people want to go along with your suggestions because compliance promises them the most fulfillment.

- *Correct difficulties before they get out of hand* If a soft answer turneth away wrath, a fast answer turneth away problems. Deal with difficulties immediately. Don't allow them to grow in the hope they'll disappear. Bite the bullet. You're the leader.

- *Watch for friction* If you notice people getting on each other's nerves, try to straighten them out. Don't let this erupt and spoil the journey for others.

- *If you don't know something, admit it* Don't try to fake your way through. If it's your first trip to an area, for example, confess this. Others will respect you for it.

- *Make people feel like individuals, even in a group* This means addressing them by name, giving them periodic recognition, and suggesting things for them personally—a book they should buy or a person they should meet.

- *Learn how to use the mike and other equipment* Don't stumble around trying to find the mike switch, and know how close to hold it to your mouth, and how high to keep the volume. If you have cassettes aboard to play, know how to work with them. This goes for any equipment you have, short of driving the coach.

- *Encourage members to participate* Draw them out. Spend some time with them, and introduce them to others. Try to get them into small groups for events on their own. Ask them to do things, from singing to assisting you with small chores.

- *Don't provide what people should have brought* Don't surrender your raincoat, razor, umbrella, or alarm clock. And don't loan people any money.

- *Keep a sharp eye on elderly or ill tour members* Other passengers may be too busy or too embarrassed to note or report such things. And the person who is not feeling well may keep quiet in order not to spoil the fun of others. That means you have to be on top of the tourists' physical conditions.

- *Always know where tour members are* Get them in the habit of making reports. Get addresses and phone numbers.
- *Have a few surprises* Games, pools, awards, impromptu entertainment, drinks on the house—these are ways to keep people happy and the tour lively.
- *You are the host* So act like one!

Mixed Groups

Tour managers agree that mixed groups work better than stag groups. Both sexes police each other. They are more polite and courteous, and they dress better under combined circumstances. It's also more fun. One European guide says that women "get more bitchy with a woman guide, especially if there are all women aboard." Maybe. But, for whatever reasons, the male-female blend works more smoothly.

Final Note

Never discuss problems in front of others. That's why the tour manager needs a private room. This is the spot for the tour manager to go over matters with the driver or courier, and the place to talk to tour members. Public chastisement is uncomfortable for everyone. Pick an appropriate time and place, and handle all confrontations tactfully.

Never discuss personal problems with tour members, like your failing marriage or your financial straits. And never bad rap your tour operator or your own agency. These are family matters.

Like Caesar's wife, the tour manager must be above suspicion. Don't let your personal flaws erode your authority. Stay away from the bottle, and the men and the women, and the race tracks, unless you can handle all of these. Keep your temper in check. Stay out of situations that could lead to problems.

In the final analysis, people on tour aren't any different than people anywhere. It's just that they are somewhat forced into unity, and the tour manager has to make this artificial situation work.

8

Special Problems and Situations

Some tour problems are beyond the control of even the most cautious tour manager. Most, however, can be anticipated and avoided. A strong argument can be made for keeping a checklist, and for having a set of detailed rules and instructions. Think about difficulties that might arise, and do a dry run on your strategy to meet them. Keep a list of local contacts in every region you visit, and know where you can turn for help.

Besides experience and careful planning, tact and common sense are valuable assets, especially when the unexpected occurs. Above all, don't panic. Too much depends on you. Maintain a calm demeanor, even if the whole tour starts to collapse about you. Getting excited is not only demoralizing to others, but also prevents you from thinking clearly and logically.

Some of the common problems a tour manager might face are covered in previous chapters. This chapter focuses on a few of these in more depth, or explores other less common happenings.

Lost and Found

Luggage Bags are one of a tour's major headaches. You can't check them too often, because they disappear at airports, between trains, and between hotels. People leave something behind, or grab the wrong bag, or put their suitcase with another tour's baggage. Travelers frequently fail to heed the warning about adding and subtracting luggage. So the count is made, and it is correct, but that's because somebody added a bag. That means someone else's luggage may be left behind. It's often the innocent who suffer. They are minus toilet articles or underwear or jackets until the lost items catch up. They may have to replace things in order to cope, or depend on the sympathy and generosity of fellow tour members.

When luggage is lost at the airport, notify the carrier and help fill out any requisite forms. The airlines will contact agents at the departure point and the next stop (in case the bags were routed ahead). The baggage claim area, of course, would have been searched thoroughly by tour manager, driver/ courier, and the individual whose bags were missing. If there were other tours departing the airport at about the same time, check on their destinations, then get in touch with them to see if they have the errant luggage. If they do, have the bags delivered to the next feasible hotel.

When you are on the move, make certain you allow sufficient time for the bags to make it to the proper hotel. Don't cut the time too close, and try to pick a hotel where you're staying more than one night. You could have the luggage following you all over Europe.

If you don't notice the loss until you get into the hotel, notify the desk clerk, bell captain, or porter. They'll search the hotel—the lobby, elevators, basement. Meanwhile the driver may be checking the coach. Tour members must be asked if they have any extra bags in their rooms, and sometimes all guests in smaller hotels may be called in an attempt to locate the cases. If these methods turn up nothing, then check out the airlines, other contemporaneous tours, and the last hotel.

Should luggage other than your own show up in your count, notify the hotel porter or bellman. If you've just arrived via air, contact the airlines (or the ship, if you just docked), telling them the flight you came on, and helping them identify the luggage.

On cruises, scour the dock area first for lost bags, then report the loss to the purser, perhaps after you have queried all your other tour members.

Tourists Suppose you are checking people in at the point of departure, and one or two persons have failed to arrive. Check first with the airline agent, just in case the people slipped by and went directly to the counter or gate. If the agent's records also show these people as absent, call the missing person's home.

No answer. Perhaps these folks are on their way. Do they have any friends who are already here? Can they tell you how the absentees planned to get to the airport? Have you looked into restaurants, bars, and rest rooms?

Now you are up against it. The plane has been called for boarding, the missing tour members still have not arrived, and you haven't been able to get in touch with them. If a representative from your travel agency is with you, turn the problem over to this person. If not, call the agency, explain the problem, have them continue to try to reach these absent members, and make arrangements for them on a later flight. If there are any additional charges, of course, the passengers must pay them.

In cases where a passenger is missing from an intermediate flight and you must leave, deposit an explanatory note with the appropriate airline ticket counter, and have this airline agent help get the tardy person to the next tour stop.

Remember that your first responsibility is to the tour as a whole. This means you'd ordinarily depart without the missing person(s). Exceptions to this rule would be if you happen to have this person's passport and he can't leave the country without it, or his tickets (although these may be left at the airline counter), or if the individual is elderly and you have no idea where he or she is. You can't merely abandon people. In these extreme cases, you'd turn the group over temporarily to some responsible tour member and join them as soon as you can. The driver/courier at the destination should be told what has happened and he or she will take over until the tour manager gets there. It should be stressed that the situation must be a real emergency, and, even then, there may be reasons why you have to go.

Sometimes a tour picks up passengers at different locations in the United States. Say that, at one of these stops, a passenger doesn't make the connection. Have this person paged at the airport. If there is no response, call the person's home, or, if known, the hotel where he or she spent the previous night. If you still come up dry, notify your agency, the tour operator, and the airline. They will try to find a way to enable the missing party to catch up with you.

If tour members become lost en route, check the hotel, fellow passengers, likely area locales and, as a last resort, notify police. Before you move on, you must know what happened to them. Perhaps some local agent or hotel staff member will take over and get the passenger routed on. Perhaps you may have to delay departure until you know the whereabouts of the missing person.

Aboard ship, the obvious place to check is the cabin, then with others who know the person, and then in the ship's public places. Enlist the aid of the purser.

If a cruise passenger who is flying to the port city fails to show up at the dock, check the airport. If time permits, and the distance is not great, you might even take a cab out there and look around. But don't endanger your own sailing. The paging system can, of course, be used with advantage both at the airport and aboard ship.

The drill is, in summary, to check the area, check with friends, check the last destination, check with authorities, and then decide whether you can leave or not. Circumstances usually dictate that you must depart. In this case, always leave some instructions to enable the lost person to rejoin you.

Passports This is a most important document and should be kept on one's person at all times. There could be routine checks by authorities, or a need for identification when financing purchases. Warn tour members not to leave their passports in rest rooms, hotel rooms, or on the airplanes or coaches.

Should a passport be lost, go over all the places where it might have been mislaid. If nothing turns up, contact the nearest American embassy. They will require proof that it is really lost, like a statement from the police, plus the witness of a person with a valid passport, perhaps yourself. Getting the new passport takes time—at least half a day.

One tour manager mentions spending his only free day in London helping a tour member get a new passport, and this person lost it again at the very next stop. Fortunately, it was located aboard the plane.

"If I had lost my passport," said the tour manager, "I think I'd have taped it to my body for the rest of the journey."

(People who run fam trips, however, will tell you that travel agents can also be careless about things like passports and other documents.)

Cash, Travelers Checks, Credit Cards Loss of these items is the responsibility of the individual, but the tour manager should know how to advise the passenger.

It's nearly impossible to recover stolen cash, unless the money is found by a scrupulous person who has the time to seek you out. If lost in a carrier, a hotel, or restaurant, you would have the tourists report this to these places. They could get lucky. But the best solution is to carry very little cash.

Everyone who watches television knows how to handle lost travelers checks. Report the loss, with the numbers of the checks to the nearest office of the issuing company. If reported on weekends or holidays, repayment may be delayed but, on weekdays, most companies will speed up refunds. American Express has an emergency service that provides everything from cash to payment of hotel bills and airline tickets. Be sure to keep the numbers of your travelers checks in several different places, so you can retrieve them when detailing the loss.

There are a number of different credit cards, and they have their own rules. Some credit card companies and banks limit liability of the owner of a stolen credit card to a certain sum, like $50, $100 or nothing. The loss must be reported immediately, so that credit may be curtailed and the thief apprehended. Tour members may also provide themselves with inexpensive insurance to cover any credit card losses.

If tour members end up without any funds because of a theft, they may phone relatives and have them send an International Money Order overseas or a postal money order in the United States. Up to $300 may also be wired to individuals in the States by relatives with Master Cards or Visa Cards.

Tickets As mentioned earlier, airline agents sometimes inadvertently pull too many tickets from a folder, leaving a few individuals short on the next leg of the journey. That's why the tour manager should be on hand when the tickets are removed, and why the ticket envelopes should be checked again before the tour manager leaves the counter.

If tickets are lost, either by you or by a passenger, the loss should be reported immediately to the carrier and to your own agency, as well as to the operator handling that portion of the tour. Substitute tickets will be provided and any difference settled by you at a later date.

Many tour managers keep all the tickets themselves. While this does place a burden on one individual, it lowers the possibility of someone in the group mislaying his or her own tickets.

Other Losses If the tour manager loses the travel vouchers, work through the driver or courier, or through the closest agent of the tour operator, to secure substitutes. Hotels may be willing to take your word (or your signed statement) and expect the vouchers later. If the driver/courier handles the vouchers, your responsibility diminishes.

Should tour members lose their health or vaccination cards, they could be detained in a foreign country. Even though these cards are used on entry into the United States, nations whose conditions require certain shots will check tourists on exit. American customs officials recommend treating this loss like a passport loss and contacting the United States embassy or consulate.

Tour members can misplace all sorts of items. False teeth, jewelry, hats, coats, glasses, cameras, and gifts. While these losses are problems for the traveler and not the tour manager, it is difficult not to get involved. Tour members expect their leader to help.

One tour director, leading his first tour recently, was accosted by a female tour member who said, in anger, "It will be your fault if I'm pregnant!" While he was puzzling out this remark, she told him she was holding him personally responsible for her loss of her handbag, which contained her birth control pills.

Illness

Passengers are expected to provide for their own medical needs. This means bringing along their own drugs, prescriptions, and diets, and making their own arrangements for any checkups or hospital stays.

The tour manager, however, will probably carry items like aspirin, cough drops, nosedrops, bandaids, and remedies for upset stomachs. Yet one must be careful about dispensing these, since resulting problems could be laid on your doorstep. A knowledge of first aid, including CPR and artificial respiration, is a handy skill. You may never need them, but people will look to you for assistance in any emergency, including illness.

Colds, headaches, nausea, and diarrhea are common ailments. At home they may be minor irritations but when traveling with a group they become serious maladies. Colds and respiratory infections spread rapidly. Try to get any sick person to a doctor as soon as possible, for that person's good as well as the health of the tour.

The person who is ill should make contact with the physician, rather than the tour manager selecting a doctor. However, if the tour member is too sick to do this, the tour manager may ask the hotel clerk or other person in authority to secure a physician. Hotels often have their own doctors, or someone they can call in an emergency. Aboard ship there is the ship's doctor and usually a small hospital or sick bay. The senior steward is the person to notify on an airplane and, if a passenger becomes ill on the coach, head for the nearest hospital or doctor's office.

Seasickness is something a tour member may prefer to handle alone, remaining in bed and shunning meals. Up to a point, this is fine, but, in the event of a prolonged illness, the tour manager should insist the person see the ship's doctor.

The list of possible medical problems is endless. Diners get food poisoning. Drinkers have hangovers. Some tourists develop allergies. Skiers get broken limbs and may need anything from an ambulance to a rescue helicopter. In addition to assuming responsibility for the securing of medical treatment, the passenger must also assume any financial obligation incurred by the visits to doctor, hospital, or pharmacist.

A tour director bringing home a group of weekend skiers had one young woman aboard with a severe case of sunburn. He treated it by breaking some vitamin E tablets and applying them to the burn areas. These entered her bloodstream and the coach had to make an emergency stop at a hospital en route. The tour manager was lucky he wasn't sued.

Here are some random comments by escorts regarding illnesses:

- "I've run into everything from helping a diabetic with insulin shots aboard a train to taking a passenger to a hospital where she had a kidney transplant."

- "One client, after flying over Greenland, told me she was pregnant, thereby nullifying her insurance. In Heidelberg she miscarried and was hospitalized, ruining that day for everyone. I got her to Milan and aboard a plane for the States—which she had to pay for."

- "Some foreign physicians are very cooperative. A couple of my people had sore throats. I phoned a physician and he ordered a pharmacist to stay open until I got there. This was in Austria, about a dozen years ago. And I remember I paid only 95 cents for the prescription."

• "An older woman on my tour kept fainting. The doctor said she shouldn't continue with us. I telephoned the States and had her son meet us in London and accompany her home. She was sick for several months. One added problem was that her grandson was with her. He was a nice kid, about twelve, and several of the other tourists wanted to take him with them, to finish the tour. But I said 'no' and sent him home. Had I allowed that, I'm sure the volunteer would have been back in a few days complaining about the inconvenience."

If possible, a sick person should be accompanied to the hospital by the tour manager, just to see that everything is settled. Relatives should always be notified. On occasion, the tour manager may even have to remain behind temporarily to make sure that the tour member is okay. Another tour member may also remain with the patient until both can rejoin the group.

When a person must be sent home, relatives should be phoned and asked for instructions. The tour manager then makes the arrangements and probably stays with the person until the flight departs. The local agent or hotel may then take over.

Prevention is always the best remedy. Travelers should have a pretour exam, and should get the shots and other medicines recommended for that particular journey. IAMAT (International Association for Medical Assistance to Travelers) and the International Health Care Service provide publications giving information on weather, sanitary conditions, required clothing, and other matters affecting health in diverse countries across the world.

International SOS Assistance provides medical help around the globe, and HOME (Help in Overseas Medical Emergencies), which has a modest membership fee, handles such things as local burial or return of the deceased to the United States, medical service or evacuation, and the repatriation of minors.

Tour managers can attend seminars on all aspects of medical attention. These courses cover emergency care, immunizations, diet, locating a physician abroad (and there is a directory of foreign physicians, by specialty), health requirements for re-entry into this country, and even how to deal with jet lag.

Although their concern is for the tour members, tour managers may also become ill. This gets particularly sticky, since the success of the tour depends to a great extent on their staying healthy. Tour managers who are under the weather should seek immediate medical attention, sneaking in rest when they can, and eating and drinking sensibly. They may also have to "play while hurt" for a while, like professional athletes.

Nobody likes to think or talk about diarrhea, but it strikes tourist and escort alike. One tour manager had a chronic case of diarrhea while in Africa. She drank boiled tea, requested extra sheets, but the malady persisted. Other members had it, too. A jungle tour aboard elephants was scheduled and she felt she must accompany the group—those who were well. Since she could hardly stray from the bathroom, she had to devise some emergency procedures. Her solution was a supply of feminine napkins, which got her through the day.

If the tour manager is unable to continue with the tour, he or she should phone the agency and a substitute will normally be provided.

When you consider that about one out of every thirty travelers abroad will be hospitalized for sickness or accident (and another twelve thousand will die) each year, this emphasizes how common sickness may be. And these statistics don't even count those who don't feel well but blunder ahead anyhow.

Handicapped travelers may encounter difficulties of their own, although there are tours catering to them, and both carriers and accommodations are becoming more sensitive to the special needs of these tourists. AMTRAK has unique facilities for the handicapped, including wider doors, specially-designed seats in the dining cars, and other innovative equipment. Bus stations are ordinarily on one level, and restrooms take the handicapped person into account. A growing number of hotels have tailored their architecture to the needs of handicapped citizens, installing ramps and other aids, like grab bars in the tub and toilet areas.

Airlines should be contacted in advance about any requirements for handicapped persons. This means notifying them of requests for things like wheelchairs or permission to board a seeing-eye dog.

It is difficult for tour managers to know everything about tour members in advance, but the more they know, the better they may advise. They can help with adjustments for the handicapped, and they may even warn persons with recent operations, including dental surgery, or with ear infections, or anemia, or advanced pregnancy, about the discomfort and possible danger of air travel.

Death

If sickness and lost luggage are traumatic for the tour manager, the thought of a member of your group dying is even more terrifying. Although the p.ospect of someone expiring on tour is a bit remote (less than one out of every 2,500 travelers die each year), the chance is always there, and the consequences invariably difficult.

- "One of our people died playing tennis in Mexico City. It was a mess getting him back to Chicago."
- "I never felt as strange as I felt getting off that plane in Omaha, carrying an urn full of ashes of one of our group."

There is no uniform procedure for dealing with the death of a tour member. Every country seems to have slightly different rules, and airlines and cruise ships are reluctant to broadcast their special routines for managing such tragedies. For the tour manager, getting specific and comprehensive information is impossible. However, there are some constants.

Should someone die overseas, the first contact should be made with the closest American embassy or consulate. The U.S. officials will then mediate with foreign officials regarding death certificates, embalming, the notifying of relatives and other matters.

Here are a few things to consider:

- In some countries you need permission from authorities in each separate geographical division through which the body passes.
- Most nations require that bodies be disposed of within twenty-four hours. This makes speed essential in getting instructions from the next-of-kin.
- If the next-of-kin opt for burial in the foreign country and later disinterment, they'd better be familiar with that nation's laws. The body may not be allowed to be moved for six months or more.
- Getting a body back to the United States can be expensive, perhaps costing several thousand dollars.
- If a body is shipped back by air, the airlines need a signed death certificate, plus a statement from the mortician or embalmer, and assurance that the coffin has been hermetically sealed. Countries like Israel and various Moslem nations prohibit embalming, so the pledge about the sealing has to suffice.

When death occurs, the tour manager should call a physician, perhaps an ambulance, and check in with the American consul or ambassador. Either the State Department official or the tour manager may then help with other arrangements, like discussing disposition of the body with relatives, or attending to burial services. If death occurs in some remote place, the burdens on the escort become even heavier.

When the next-of-kin request that the body be shipped back to the United States, they will be charged according to distance and the weight of the coffin. Deceased persons have freight priority, and that adds to the expense incurred. This payment must be made before the body leaves foreign soil. Relatives can arrange such payment via the State Department in Washington, which will transfer the funds to their foreign consulate. In some cases, shipment may be delayed until the local government is satisfied that the deceased left no unpaid bills.

(One thing the tour manager might do in the pretour meeting is tactfully suggest that each passenger leave written instructions about what should be done in case of death overseas. This might be part of the person's will.)

When a person dies on an airplane, the crew will usually cover the body with a blanket but not move it. The pilot then calls ahead to the nearest airport, relaying a message to authorities there (either in this country or abroad), setting in motion the things mentioned above, like clearing local regulations and contacting next-of-kin. Other passengers are generally disembarked before the ambulance takes the body from the plane.

When death occurs on a cruise, there are three ways this is handled. Burial at sea remains a possibility, but more common are transfer of the body to an airplane at the next port for the flight home, or the keeping of the body in the ship's cold storage until the cruise is complete. While, at first blush, it seems a trifle bizarre for a widow or widower to continue the vacation with a spouse lying below, this is often done. Among other things, it saves considerable expense and red tape. Ships like the QE II have their own mortuaries and can handle all emergencies aboard.

Through all of these grim arrangements, the tour manager must not only remain calm, but must also prevent the atmosphere from turning into one large funeral procession. A Canadian tour manager did this so well, only the dead person's roommate on a three-day British Columbia tour knew about the death. This happened on the first day and the other members did not yet know their fellow passengers. The death was handled with quiet and dispatch.

Crime

Social critics used to observe that the only place in the world where citizens were not safe on the street was in America. That was changed. Other cities across the globe now have higher crime rates and represent dangers to travelers. Whether you are conducting a tour of Americans or visitors through our country, or taking Americans elsewhere, caution is the byword.

This means locking hotel doors securely, knowing where the key to your room is (preferably at the desk), maintaining a watchful eye on your purse or wallet. Purses should be in your lap in a public place and not in the seat next to you, and firmly in your hands even when touring museums or playing the slot machines. For men, inside pockets are best and the wallet material that makes removal difficult is an added safeguard. Some law officers instruct tourists to walk against the traffic flow if you think you're being trailed by a car, to drop your wallet or purse in a mailbox if closely pursued, and to head for a police station, fire station, hospital or hotel.

Tour managers must confer with local guides about safe and unsafe areas and warn their charges about such dangers. All crimes, like thefts and assaults, must be communicated to local authorities, and must be included in the tour manager's report.

If it seems necessary in certain locales, members may be alerted to prostitution and solicitation. Some nations have severe penalties for engaging in sex for hire, and the traveler will find this is not just another lark in a convention city. For that and other reasons, it's best to keep moving if propositioned.

If there are other customs and laws which may be different, the tour member must be warned, especially about what they do during free time. Perhaps no one is allowed to roam without an assigned guide; perhaps certain areas are off limits to photographers; perhaps there are dress codes or religious regulations with penalties for disobedience. There may also be temptations to engage in black market activities for goods or money. All of these are taboo.

Traffic laws could also come into play, especially if tour members elect to hire an automobile on free days. Be sure they know things like legal speed limits, the meaning of road signs (which are becoming more universal), parking restrictions, insurance limitations, and, in a few countries, the existence of portside driving.

Even pedestrians have to be wary. Many come from cities where jay-walking is tolerated because it's the only way to make it across busy streets. In some nations (and in some American cities) this behavior could result in a fine.

Political Problems

Never isolate yourself from local happenings. If you know you are entering a troubled area, call ahead to the hotel or to the embassy and get a reading on the current situation. Many guides suggest talking with porters rather than hotel management, since the latter tend to be more sanguine. If things look too volatile, you should cancel reservations in that locale and secure accommodations elsewhere.

If you do find yourself in an area where there is unrest, political or otherwise, caution tour members to avoid rallies and demonstrations and, in fact, to return quickly to the hotel if anything seems to be happening. No tourists should participate in marches, picket lines, assemblies, or even informal debates. Play it cool.

Should armed conflict arise while the tour is in a specific locality, call the embassy or consulate for instructions. They may suggest removal to a rural area or evacuation. While waiting for these changes, the group must stay together and out of danger.

Bob English of Peter Travel, was caught in Cairo in 1973 when a joint Egyptian-Syrian attack was made on Israel. A high percentage of English's tour members were Jewish. He called his group together, contacted the American embassy, and succeeded in having the tour evacuated by ship.

Another tour under the direction of twenty-four year veteran Charles Kissane was in Angkor Wat, Cambodia, when all borders were suddenly closed and all transportation frozen. Kissane managed to secure vehicles to get his group out by road. It took a stiff bribe for the border officials.

Incidentally, most brochures and itineraries make it clear that political upheavals, armed conflicts, and acts of God are not the responsibility of the tour operators. Any expenses involved in getting out of these tight situations must be borne by the tour members themselves.

Acts of God

First of all, tours should shun areas where some natural disturbance is imminent. There's no sense in continuing on to the Florida Keys if hurricane warnings have been posted, or trekking to some South Seas paradise during a period of volcanic activity. However, if you find yourself on the spot when calamity strikes, you usually employ for the group the same precautions you would take as an individual.

You find appropriate shelter from hurricanes and tornadoes, locating a spot, preferably underground, with strong walls and overhead protection. Earthquakes also require shelter, trying to stay clear of structures that may collapse and injure you. In all cases, get the group swiftly to safety, keep them together, and maintain calm. Once the danger is past, summon aid.

When a flood threatens, get the tour members to higher ground. Be firm and serious, and allow no procrastination.

Genevieve Smith of Green Carpet Tours recalls:

"Several years ago on one of our Alaska tours, the group overnighted at Fireside Inn, Milepost 543, British Columbia. During the night a flash flood damaged two bridges leaving the group stranded out in the middle of nowhere, as there were no alternate roads. The telephone was out of service, so the escort could not advise Portland of this situation. He explained to the group that he had been advised by a highway crew the bridges should be repaired in approximately twenty-four hours. At his request they said they would advise via their radio communication system the onward hotels about the situation. After receiving the message, one of the hotel managers called Portland to advise us of the situation. In the meantime, the group was playing bingo, bridge, and eating too often, thanks to the escort who had skillfully implanted the thought 'enjoy this unique adventure.' And this is what they did! Although they were detained thirty hours they completed the tour without further mishap. On the final day of the tour the escort received a sizable gratuity and we received no complaints."

FIRE

Fire is always a concern, especially when staying in strange hotels. There are numerous booklets available on what to do in case of fire. The tour manager should secure one and master it.

When the tour enters any hotel, and after check-in has been accomplished, review the alarm system with the desk clerk. Is it a siren, bell, or what? Locate fire escapes and stairwells and suggest that tour members do the same. If there are fire alarms or other fire fighting equipment, note locations. Tell tour members to count the number of doors between their rooms and the stairwells or fire escapes. They could be caught in heavy smoke and have to feel their way to safety.

Tourists should also check around their own rooms, noting whether or not there is a ledge, how the windows open, and where they are in relationship to adjacent buildings. All of this must be accomplished without frightening the guests unnecessarily.

Hotel room keys should be left in the same spot each night, so they can be picked up in the dark. If you have to leave the room because of fire, don't waste time packing clothes. Put on your shoes (which should also be handy) in case you must walk through broken glass. A small flashlight would also be a sensible thing to pack for occasions like this. Guests who leave their rooms during fire should take their keys with them. The stairwells could be blocked by smoke or flames, and the person may have to come back to the room.

Manuals instruct persons caught in fires to do the following:

- Phone the desk and see what is happening. You could be the first to detect the presence of smoke.

- Feel the door to see if it's hot. If it is, don't open it. Stay inside awaiting rescue. If the door is cool, open and close it rapidly (to prevent suction and to keep smoke from getting at belongings left behind). Move toward the predetermined fire exits, turning on any alarms you en-counter en route. Walk or crawl, depending on the amount of smoke. Keep low and close to the wall. Never take the elevator.

- Your aim is to get below the fire (since heat and smoke rise) but, if you can't get down, go to the roof—a secondary safety area.
- Once the fire is underway, you may be better off staying in your room, with wet towels wedged into the door cracks. Fill the bathtub with water in case the water pressure goes off. You'll need the water to wet more towels. Air conditioning and heating systems should be turned off, and windows may be opened slightly. Use the drapes (which are a hazard anyway) to signal location, then lie down (to escape carbon monoxide gas) and await rescue. As a last resort, the windows may be broken if this offers a chance of escape.
- Some tour managers agree on a place to meet after evacuating the building. This makes it easier to count heads and check on who is safely out. Neither the tour manager nor other members should re-enter the burning building to find someone. Leave that to the professionals.
- Remind tour members to check all these things themselves, and to avoid foolish behavior, like smoking in bed.
- Aboard ships and airplanes, the crew handles demonstrations and drills which will be employed in case of fire or other disaster.

Delays

Transportation can be delayed for a variety of reasons, from weather to strikes, from equipment malfunctions to road conditions. This happens to airplanes, ships, trains, coaches, even taxicabs, despite their precautions to guard against such failures. When such delays occur, try to determine how long they will be, and then use your ingenuity to make the wait as comfortable as possible for your passengers. Level with your tour members about the situation and don't lie about the delay time.

If a coach breaks down, the driver will summon a mechanic or a replacement. If feasible, the passengers can wait in a nearby town or hotel, or they may have to stay aboard the bus. Some latitude may be allowed for strolling around the vicinity of the breakdown, but don't let passengers wander off, and keep them out of danger areas.

With train delays, there is usually little you can do, unless the train remains in the station and you can disembark people. With ships, the situation is generally eased. Since the ship is really a floating hotel, tour members can be more comfortable and also find things to do. Of course, in both situations problems could multiply with heat or air-conditioning off and -electricity not working.

Airline delays seem to cause most concern. Whole itineraries may have to be rescheduled; accommodations could be lost or replaced; food must be provided; other carriers and suppliers need to be reached. It can be a mess. Stateside, even though inconvenienced, airline delays are rarely as big a headache as overseas hangups.

Tour manager Charles Kissane was once stranded with his group in a remote area of Afghanistan after their chartered aircraft broke down.

"We were there for two days. I had to arrange for sleeping in a large barn, and I think I got every egg in the village. We subsisted on bread and eggs. Because of the delay we missed our international flight from Kabul to Teheran, and had to make alternate arrangements on a line that had very few flights. In Teheran the hotel had cancelled our rooms because we hadn't shown up. The hotel was now full, so I had to call all over town to get one or two rooms in a dozen different places."

Barbara Leonard of Discovery Tours found herself stranded with her group when a ferry service wasn't operating and couldn't take them to their hotel across the water. While the courier took tour members to a museum, the tour manager worked on both the ferry service and alternate accommodations. Finally she contacted the ferry authorities and got her group across.

"That's when the company's emergency allowance is used," she adds.

When Dick Linde, a minister with considerable tour experience, found himself in Tokyo's airport with five hours to kill, he knew there wasn't sufficient time to get into town and back, but he didn't want to spend these hours cooped up in a small lounge. So he rented a room in a nearby hotel and tossed a party for the tour members.

Situations vary. Groups have been caught on the runway and forced to remain aboard for several warm and boring hours. Here's a real test for the tour manager, who should circulate among the tourists, radiating as much good will as can be mustered. Drinks may be served under these conditions— anything to take the passengers' minds off their troubles.

Since ultimate responsibility rests with tour managers, these individuals must insist that carriers live up to agreements to provide adequate substitutes.

David Davidowitz of Vagabond Tours for the Deaf hit a snag on his first escorted tour in 1966. With thirty-four deaf tour members, he reached London airport to find thousands of Americans sleeping all over the place. His tour's airline was the only carrier not on strike but, when they tried to board the plane, they were turned back. Their seats had been sold.

"An airlines official offered us one more day in London. I refused. These deaf people had to get back to their jobs. I told the airline agent to get my seats back. The flight was held up for four hours. Four airline officials pleaded with me about babies and the elderly. Finally I told him if he wanted to pay a million dollars because of loss of jobs, that was his worry."

Then they offered Davidowitz a bribe, which he turned down, leading to the airline capitulating. The deaf group got their seats, infuriating the other passengers.

Davidowitz said, "We came over with them, and we're going home with them."

His clients witnessed the entire scenario. The tale of his standing up for them "spread across the U.S.A.," he says.

Miscellaneous

There are numerous other things which can go wrong. Some are serious; some are humorous. Your American tour operator may promise one thing, but the foreign representative has a different impression and this leads to confusion. Lack of communication with suppliers at all levels can cause difficulty.

Loretta Cutler of Travel & Transport arrived at her German hotel the evening of America's moon walk. The town was filled with German citizens who came to see the historic occasion in the local hotels. The hotel manager said he couldn't supply the single rooms they'd promised, but offered enough rooms for people to share. All but one refused to share. After a couple of hours of fruitless protesting, Ms. Cutler had to find other rooms in the city.

When traveling between countries on a multination trip, passage through customs can sometimes be difficult. You may get caught up in a concentrated drug search, or arrive the day after a bombing or riot and be subject to extensive scrutiny. Relax, and think and act sensibly. Keep tour members from irritating local customs officers.

"One of my passengers refused to let Russian officials open her handbag," said one tour manager," and they got a little rough with her. She had some film in there which really wasn't any problem, but she just insisted on her rights. They arrested her and I had to get her out. It was a bad scene, and we missed our plane. The other tourists could have killed her."

One a more humorous note, a tour leader writes:

"Once our rooms were not ready when the tour arrived, so I bought everyone a drink in the hotel bar. The delay continued, so I suggested that the people roam around for about an hour while I watched their carry-on items in the bar. After everyone had returned and claimed their belongings, one item remained—a man's coat with several pairs of women's panties stuffed in the pockets."

What a Consulate/Embassy Can and Can't Do

Although the American embassy or consulate is the first refuge in major difficulties, they can't do everything.

Consulates can provide a ninety-day passport replacement, supply a list of

English-speaking physicians or other professionals (without recommending any specific person), monitor absentee voting, warn travelers about war and other disorders, locate missing family members, extend a repatriation loan for direct return to the United States, and they may even offer the services of a notary public. The consulate, however, won't make loans, cash personal checks, hold or forward mail, or make hotel reservations.

Travelers Through America

This chapter concentrates on Americans going abroad on tour, but there are also tours in the United States which involve those from outside our borders. Most of the advice in these pages still applies, except that contact would be made with representatives of their governments in cases of emergency.

9

The Return Trip and Afterwards

As the time to return home nears, the tour manager must start thinking about re-entry into the United States, or, if the tour is enjoying this nation's hospitality, about sending our guests home. In either case, reconfirm space at least forty-eight hours before departure. Also check on flight and sailing times, on type of equipment being used, on meals aloft or afloat, and on any connecting flights that must be met. Also confer on times the group should be at the airport or pier, and discuss any special regulations affecting the homeward journey.

If members wish to extend their tour, this is, of course, at their own expense and direction. The tour manager or tour operator may assist in making these additional arrangements, which should be concluded well in advance of the departure date.

Tour members may wish to complete last minute shopping, so it's smart to allow for some blocks of free time in the final days. It's also wise to book a hotel not too distant from the airport or docks. You don't want to spend hours trying to get to the point of departure, particularly if you have an early flight or sailing.

Another intelligent move is to schedule some event, like a dinner (or cabaret or play), the evening prior to departure. This adds a pleasant punctuation mark to the trip, and also allows you to see that all tour members are accounted for. Don't make this a late night; just something to top off the excursion. On the coach going back to the hotel (or sometime before the tour members retire for the night), go over the next day's itinerary, reminding people not to pack their passports (or health cards), but to have them handy for inspection, counseling them on what they can expect en route and at customs, and repeating the instructions about rising and departing.

Checking In

Allow plenty of time to get to the airport, and sufficient time to handle matters once you get there. Arriving two hours ahead of departure is advisable.

Bring the passengers into the terminal and locate them in one area in the lounge. Ask them to wait there until you check all of them in. The driver and porters will be unloading the luggage and transferring it to the airline counter. Tour members should not leave their carry-on luggage unattended at this time, but should request that another member watch it if they go to the rest rooms. This may be the occasion for farewells to the driver and/or courier. They'll want to move the coach. Usually these individuals visit the waiting tour members to say their goodbyes.

The airlines may or may not weigh baggage. If they do weigh it, they may accept a total figure divided by the number of tour members. Anyone in violation of the weight or number rules must pay any difference personally, and even though your experience tells you such charges are infrequently made, don't assure the tour members that excesses will be no problem.

When you go the airline counter, you'll be carrying the tickets and the passports you've just collected from tour members. The agent there will match passport to ticket, perhaps examine health cards, pull tickets, weigh and tag luggage, make out boarding passes and then return to you the ticket envelopes, boarding passes, passports and baggage claim checks. The passports and boarding passes go to tour members; you retain the ticket envelopes, especially if some tickets remain for domestic connections, and the claim checks. If someone wants the ticket folder later as a souvenir, fine, and you may want to give baggage checks to any individuals who are leaving the tour in the United States before you reach the final destination.

As before, make certain that the agent hasn't pulled too many tickets, and be sure that the bags are tagged for the proper destinations in the States. Regardless of final routing, the bags will come off at customs and will then be returned to the ongoing airline. If you have persons going to different American cities, double check their baggage tags.

If there are any final instruction persons should be given, like changes in flight times, the departure gate number, the type of aircraft being used, the sailing time and cabin arrangements, the meal schedule, and the like, do this now. If some free times remains, let tour members visit shops or restaurants or bars in the vicinity, but schedule an early time for them to be back in this spot so you can lead them to the gate.

Should this airport or pier feature duty free goods, the carrier usually allows ample time for passengers to shop. Travelers from Dublin to New York, for example, will deplane at Shannon airport for an hour in its huge duty-free shop.

If airline officials permit early boarding for tour groups, take advantage of this. And try to make amends now for any inferior seats on the way over; give these people the choice seats, again trying to keep spouses and friends together. Board last yourself, counting everyone aboard, and counting them again as soon as you are settled.

Return Journey

The trip back is much like the trip over, except that the group will be both more tired and more stimulated. When you can, visit with each of the people, gathering their impressions, and sharing their experiences. This might also be your last opportunity to treat them to a drink.

Some tour members may need help with the debarkation or custom declaration cards. Assist them in filling these out. Be sure you know the proper responses to questions about customs. For example:

- Each traveler is allowed an exemption on goods purchased out of the country. This amount ($300 in 1982) is figured on the fair market value of those goods in that country. Tourists coming from certain American possessions may be permitted double that amount. Families traveling together may pool their purchases and exemptions. A husband and wife with two children, for instance, could bring home goods worth $1,200 without paying any tax or duty.

- To qualify for this exemption, you must have been outside the United States for at least 48 hours, and you can't claim twice within the space of 30 days.

- To merit an exemption, the articles must be with you. Those shipped home are subject to duty. Items of clothing, and jewelry, which you may have used during the tour are still subject to the legal limit.

- If you're over 21, you can carry home one exempt quart of liquor, and not more than 100 cigars or 200 cigarettes. If you take from the foreign country more than $5,000 in currency or other monetary instruments, you must file a special report.

- Unless you have special permission (and few tourists do), you are forbidden to bring into the country any fruits, vegetables, plants, seeds, flowers, meats, or pets. There's a danger of disease to crops, animals, and humans from some of these items.
- If the tour member doesn't have goods in excess of $300, there is no need to itemize.

Never advise any one to do anything illegal, and don't condone such practices if suggested. True, people do get by with some illegalities, but you never want to be in a position of countenancing such behavior.

Customs

Passage through customs is always something of a problem. Tourists are tired and frightened, even when they have no reason to be nervous. You must remind them they are on their own when clearing customs, and that you can't really assist them. Somehow these frail, elderly folks, laden down with packages, make it through.

If you can, get off first, clear the initial passport check, and head for the customs hall. You may be able to round up carts for the rest of your group and assist them in loading their gear as it comes off the conveyors. Again, try to get through quickly yourself (if your luggage cooperates), and then arrange for a place to meet, and for porters to handle the luggage and transfer it to the proper airline.

You can't hurry or hassle the customs officers. Let them do their job. Sometimes they open everything; other times the search is more cursory. But the options are theirs, not yours. Once everyone has cleared customs, paid any duty owed, and assembled outside the area, keep them together as you secure ground transportation. If the domestic terminal is close, you may decide to walk it, but a bus is more likely. Pay any porters and also pay for the ground transport service.

This may be the place where some members separate and head off to other cities. Take time for a proper farewell, and agree to contact them about any plans for a reunion of tour members.

Once you have reached the domestic terminal, count heads again, and check your passengers in. If there is a long wait between flights, allow travelers time off, arranging to meet well ahead of departure. If time is short, take them right to the gate. They can now put away their passports and, if you wish, you can hand them their ticket envelopes. All they really need at this point are their boarding passes.

Home

When you reach your final destination disembark first and help others off. Go to the baggage claim area, checking the carousel number in advance.

Travel agency representatives should be on hand to help greet passengers, and you may want to make a short, oral report to them on the trip. Your duties are not really over until all baggage has been claimed and the last tour member has left the terminal. If luggage is lost, help the tour member fill out the proper form. If all goes well, say your goodbyes and head home yourself.

Follow-up

Some cleanup chores remain.

- Some travel agencies send evaluation cards to tour members, asking for their impressions of the tour and the personnel in charge. They may mail these back, with or without a signature. Sometimes these may be circulated during the return flight or voyage, or before members leave the baggage claim area. It works better to mail them.

- The tour manager may send a short note to tour members shortly after coming home, thanking them for their cooperation, and discussing any future gatherings. Responses of tour members sometimes provide excellent copy for future brochures, but don't force this; let it be spontaneous.

- Add the names and addresses of tour members to the agency mailing list, and also gather any other names they care to supply.

- Complete your expense forms, retaining a copy for your own files, and return any unused funds.

- Fill out the tour manager's report, including highlights of the journey and any untoward events, such as illness, breakdowns, delays, itinerary changes, or tour member dismissals.

- Include a critique of the hotels and restaurants, the entertainment, the carriers, the tour operator, and the performance of the various personnel. Be specific, since generalities don't help much, and don't focus on the negative only. Positive suggestions also aid in planning future trips.

- As soon as possible, dispatch thank-you letters to suppliers, hotels, tour operator personnel, and others. You may also want to drop a longer letter to tour members, including names and addresses of people they may have met, and addresses of shops and the like. This may be the place to establish a date for the tour members' reunion.

Manager's Report

Some travel agencies and tour operators have their own special forms to be filled out; others leave that to the tour manager. It makes little difference, as long as the essential information is there.

There are three essential elements in this report:

1. A diary-like list of events, particularly those things which are unusual, like a departure from the itinerary, special local problems, illness and other things.

   Example:

   MAY 16: Arrived late to Florence and had to pass up half of museum tour. Bus breakdown delayed us three hours. Also had to find a physician for Ms. Holly who had been bothered by dizzy spells. Group was good about the changes. Ms. Holly was able to continue with the tour.

2. A critique of hotels, restaurants and services. These will be helpful for future trips, and also provide information for other agency personnel.

   Example:

   MAY 22: Das Kaserne Hotel is small but very clean, and the staff is friendly and accommodating. Meals here are superb, the best of the trip. The west side of the hotel is near the Autobahn and that makes sleeping difficult. I'd always ask for rooms on the east or north. The hotel is also located quite a distance from the main Berlin shopping area.

3. A complete rundown on all expenses. It helps to carry a small notebook to record expenses as they are committed. These may be transferred to other forms that evening. Record expenses in the local currency, with conversion rates, and all the figures can later be translated into dollars.

   Example:

MAY 14:	Lunch in Lyons	28 francs
	Phone calls	7 francs
	Wine for Douglas anniversary	172 francs
	Admissions to winery	30 francs
	Dinner at hotel	105 francs
		342 francs

The tour manager may want to report separately on the tour operator and this operator's personnel. And there could be other items which require more space and more details. There is flexibility for this.

Reunion

Getting together at least once again after the trip is a nice idea. Some tour groups meet annually, and some members take several tours together after this initial shared experience.

First, set a convenient date for the reunion, avoiding any important conflicts, and staying clear of normal vacation times.

Then select a locale. This could be the home of one of the tour members, or your home, or the home of an agency VIP. It could be the recreation center of an apartment complex where a tour member lives. Or the hall of some company that provides the facilities free for local groups. Be certain that this hall has no restrictions against things like liquor. The site must also be large enough, convenient, and at least marginally attractive. Invitations should be issued at least two weeks ahead of the event, and preferably a month. Spouses should be included.

Try to come up with a theme that matches the geography of the tour. This may mean national colors, pennants, maps, posters, even native costumes. The food, too, can take on the national character—pasta, gyros sandwiches, rice pilaf, trifle, Irish coffee. Have some records or tapes playing appropriate music to set the mood.

The program somewhat runs itself. People will be happy to see one another and they'll be exchanging stories. Have them bring their photos or slides. These should be circulated and you might run a contest to judge the best pictures in several categories. Be sure you have the right projectors on hand, with extension cords, empty trays, an extra bulb, and a screen.

Occasionally, the courier from overseas may be able to join you. Some of them make promotional tours through the United States and you could schedule your reunion around their visit.

Tour members who are unable to come, primarily because they live out of town, might be phoned and given an opportunity to chat with some of their old friends. Ultimately, you wrap it up, but keep these people posted on future trips, and on other local events that may extend the experience they enjoyed.

Index